Recollections of Pitt County

Roger Kammerer

Published by The History Press
Charleston, SC 29403
www.historypress.net

Copyright © 2006 by Roger Kammerer
All rights reserved

Cover Image: Courtesy of Judy Nobles Lewis

First published 2006

Manufactured in the United States

ISBN 978.1.54020.411.0

Library of Congress Cataloging-in-Publication Data

Kammerer, Roger E.
Recollections of Pitt County, North Carolina / Roger Kammerer.
p. cm.
ISBN 978-1-59629-132-4 (alk. paper)
1. Pitt County (N.C.)--History--Anecdotes. I. Title.
F262.P6K36 2006
975.6'44--dc22
2006009238

Notice: The information in this book is true and complete to the best of our knowledge. It is offered without guarantee on the part of the author or The History Press. The author and The History Press disclaim all liability in connection with the use of this book.

All rights reserved. No part of this book may be reproduced or transmitted in any form whatsoever without prior written permission from the publisher except in the case of brief quotations embodied in critical articles and reviews.

Contents

Acknowledgements	7
Pitt County's Six Courthouses	11
A History of the Town Common	17
Pitt County Places in 1921	22
Have You Ever Heard Tale Of…?	25
Yonder She Comes Rounding the Point: A History of Steamboats on the Tar	30
Dr. B. Brown Williams, Mesmerist and Clairvoyant	39
The Bridges Over the Tar River	43
ECU Founder's Day Remembered	48
Pitt County in the Movies	52
Dr. David Richard Wallace, Eminent Psychiatrist of Texas	56
The Bomber That Flew Under the Bridge	59
A History of Bensboro	62
Local Mineral Springs and Amuzu Park	66
Boston Napoleon Bonapart Boyd, Self-Made Man	70
Floods, Freezes and Flying Objects	73
The Old Brick Store	76
Remembering the Old Restaurants	79
Jesse James's Brother and the Treasure of Yankee Hall	84
Spanish Flu Epidemic of 1918	87
Dr. George Hatem, Legendary Figure in China's Public Health	91
Tales of the Odd and Unusual	94
The Imperial Tobacco Company	99

Local Valentines Traditions	103
Tales from the Civil War	106
Rambling in the 1960s: Entertainment in Greenville	110
Tales of the Halloween Season	116
Images of Pitt County	119
About the Author	125

ACKNOWLEDGEMENTS

Recollections of Pitt County, North Carolina is a small compilation of the several hundred articles I have written for the *Greenville Times* since 1984. I am truly grateful to Susan Daughtry, the owner and editor of the *Greenville Times*, for letting me have the freedom to write on any aspect of Pitt County's and Greenville's history that I wanted to and for continuing my column. I have truly enjoyed sharing the stories I have heard and the historical gems that come to light every month. In my articles I have tried to show everything from the basic struggle to live to the kinship across the generations. To give a sense of place, made up of uncommon folks with a no-nonsense practicality and ingenuity, of Southern graciousness, and of course, an unending sense of humor.

I am truly indebted to so many people. My heartfelt thanks to my friend Elizabeth Ross for her willingness to help me with computers, editing, scanning pictures and most of all guidance. Her skillful research on Pitt County families and history has helped preserve so much of our past.

I would also like to thank another partner in crime, that redheaded powerhouse, Candace Pearce. She has done so much to get the movers and shakers of our area to preserve what we have left of our past in Greenville and in the county. She and I had the opportunity to publish a photographic book of Greenville back in 2001 and create a photographic archive from which several images in this book were taken.

Another friend, of whom I could not have done without over the years, is Mr. John F. Moye, a Southern gentleman whose fascinating bits of history, facts, lore and humor have kept me running for a pen to write it all down. His willingness to share his memories, his photographs

This is the scene in front of the country store of J.J. Oakley & Sons taken about 1905. The store was formerly located at the intersection of what is now Black-Jack and Gaskins Roads. *Courtesy of Arleta Cox Wood.*

and his knowledge of Pitt County back roads and people makes him a living reference.

I also received great help from my friends Matthew Cook, a Greenville graphic artist, and Rick Smiley, a computer guru, who I put upon for scanning my old photographs every time a new one is uncovered.

I owe a great deal to the Pitt County Historical Society for their constant support of me and my work, especially Liz Sparrow, Sandra Hunsucker, Jerri Sutton, Evelyn L. Boyette, Greenville Banks and Mary H. Everett. And I want to express my pride in my association with my friends and fellow history buffs of the Pitt County Family Researchers, Inc. From them I have learned so much more about Pitt County.

I have to also thank the people at the places I have haunted since my interest in Pitt County history began back in 1980. They have shared so much. At the Eastern Division of Archives and History in Greenville, Stan Little and Scott Power. At the North Carolina Collection in the J.Y. Joyner Library, East Carolina University, there is Maury York and Fred Harrison. In the Manuscript Collection in the J.Y. Joyner Library, there is the indomitable Martha Elmore. Their knowledge, assistance and patience have been invaluable.

Acknowledgements

This book would be less appealing if it were not for the photographs. Many thanks to Judy Nobles Lewis for sharing her old Greenville postcard collection; Bob Newton of Farmville, North Carolina, for sharing his collection of train photographs and Gay Bland Davenport, Patsy Styron, Libby D. Turner and Buddy Waters for sharing interesting family photographs.

Most of the information for the articles in this book came from personal interviews with local residents; research at the North Carolina Archives in Raleigh: the North Carolina Collection and the Manuscript Collection in the J.Y. Joyner Library at East Carolina University; and the several Greenville newspapers on microfilm, including the *Eastern Reflector*, *Daily Reflector* and the *Greenville Daily News*.

I hope a little of the great heritage of Pitt County comes alive for you when you read this book and both the native and the newcomer learn something new. Thanks!

Pitt County's Six Courthouses

The courthouse and the courthouse square pervades the North Carolina townscape, and since the beginning has played an unusually important role in the region's historical development. The courthouse has been by tradition the commercial center of any town. Business of all types was conducted on the square and in some counties the market house stood adjacent to the courthouse. The courthouse is often one of the county's most opulent structures and a symbol of local pride and history. The following is a small history of Pitt County's six courthouses, each leaving a legacy of their own as the hub about which county life symbolically revolved.

In 1760, there was a petition to the State Assembly stating that Beaufort County was so large, it was difficult for some inhabitants to attend the "courts, general musters and other public meeting" and they wanted another county formed. The government created a new county named in honor of William Pitt, the British secretary of state. The act establishing the county of Pitt took effect on January 1, 1761, and also called for the construction of a courthouse, prison and stocks on the land of John Hardee on the south side of the Tar River near Hardee's Chapel.

The new county of Pitt had no money to build a courthouse so John Hardee donated the use of his house as the courthouse. John Hardee's house was a large, two-story frame building with a massive double chimney of Flemish bond on one end. It was located east on Highway 33, nearly across from the present-day entrance to Brook Valley Country Club. The house remained standing until it was torn down in

This is a drawing of the first Pitt County Courthouse as it appeared about 1920. This interesting house was later used as a tenant house, school and pack house until it was finally torn down in 1926. *Courtesy of the author.*

January 1926. In September 1930, the Greenville Patriots chapter of the Daughters of the American Republic erected a marker stone at the site of this old courthouse and unveiled it on October 25 with a huge ceremony and parade.

Evidence shows that the second courthouse was built in Martinsborough (now Greenville) about 1776. According to an act of the State Assembly in 1775, George Evans, Charles Forbes, Henry Ellis, Benjamin May and William Roberson were appointed commissioners to contract with workmen for the removal of the courthouse, prison and stocks to Martinsborough. Court was held in the house of John Leslie until the new courthouse was finished.

In 1789, Pitt County petitioned the State Assembly to allow them to lay an annual tax on its inhabitants to build a new courthouse, prison and stocks. James Armstrong, Shadrach Allen, John Moye, Arthur Forbes, Samuel Simpson, Benjamin Bell and William Blount were appointed commissioners to receive the tax money collected by the sheriff. They were to superintend the building of the new courthouse and to dispose of the old one when the new one was completed. Using later statements made by the Pitt County clerk in legal documents, it is understood that the Pitt County papers in his office only went back to 1792. Apparently the old records from 1761–91 in the clerk's office were burned or thrown out before the new courthouse was built in 1792. Somehow the Pitt County deed books have survived, apparently being stored in another building or in the register's home.

We know from records that the third courthouse, built about 1792, was a frame building sitting on high brick pillars with a long flight of steps up the front. This was a popular style of courthouse at the time and several North Carolina counties had the same design. This courthouse was said to have been situated on the courthouse square at the corner of Evans and Third Streets, facing Evans Street. An interesting event happened in September 1901 when heavy rains led to a cave-in of the sidewalk on the Third Street side of the building now housing the Courtside Café. Old-timers then recalled that it was the old public well that supplied water for this courthouse and the old jail that sat where Courtside Café now sits.

On June 25, 1833, George Eason, James Blow, Bryan Grimes, Goold Hoyt and John Norcott, commissioners to build a new courthouse, advertised that they would receive building proposals until September 1. The commissioner, Goold Hoyt, won the contract and in 1834 he built a large, two-story brick building, fifty-two by forty feet, which was supposedly fireproof. Goold Hoyt, who owned the leading hotel in Greenville, created a brickyard behind his hotel to make the courthouse bricks. The wood of the old courthouse was sold to Marshall Dickinson, who used it to build another building on a lot; this lot is now located on south Pitt Street near the old Coca Cola Bottling works. The brick pillars with the old floor as a roof remained standing for many years as a public market.

This new fourth courthouse, which sat in the middle of Evans Street, was described in old newspapers at the time as "being plain" and "tolerable." It served the county until the dark rainy morning of January 7, 1858, when it burned to the ground. The fire consumed all the records since 1792, except the deed books in the register's office and a trial docket dated September 1823 to March 1858 from the county clerk's office. The estimated loss to Pitt County at the time was $6,000. The courthouse was supposedly burned by a man named Croom, from Tennessee, who was trying to destroy a will. Circumstantial evidence pointing to him as the culprit was so strong that the grand jury found a true bill against him, but he was never brought to trial for the crime.

Soon after the fire the Pitt County justices appointed a committee to adopt a plan for a new fifth courthouse and contract with someone to build it. The committee procured a building plan supposedly from a leading architectural firm in Baltimore, Maryland, and by August 1858 awarded the contract to Dabney Cosby of Raleigh, North Carolina, for the then-snug sum of $12,000. John W. Cosby, son of Dabney Cosby and also a well-known architect, was to superintend the work. Cosby later proposed certain modifications to the original plan of the courthouse, which the justices of court agreed to. After about six months, the justices inspected a draft of the proposed modifications and rejected them and notified Dabney Cosby to give bond and security within three weeks that he would execute the work according to the original plan or forfeit all claims to the contract. Cosby ignored the notice and went to the public square in Greenville and, without consulting with the building committee on the designated site, proceeded with a large number of workmen to erect a brick building. The building commissioners complained to the justices of the county court that Cosby was not building the courthouse to contract, it was being built of inferior materials and it was "a specimen of architecture...unworthy of the county of Pitt." The county court filed an injunction against Dabney Cosby and had the work stopped. The justices took the case to the North Carolina Supreme Court. The final outcome is unclear, though it is known that another contractor was hired and he too had a falling out with the county justices. It appears the whole disagreement about the courthouse concerned the architectural style. This fifth courthouse sat unfinished for years, though the court began using the first floor in February 1863. The shingle roof was completed in 1861 and the building was not finished until 1877. Dabney Cosby was remembered for many years afterwards by the people of Greenville.

It was reported that during the lawless days of Reconstruction this fifth courthouse was the scene of riots and shootings. In January 1867, it was reported that a band of desperados had entered the clerk's office in the courthouse and destroyed a large number of records and legal documents. In October 1887, Ben F. Patrick offered for sale an antique relic: a two-horse wagon made by Jim Nelson about 1847. It had been bought by Cosby for $190 and used to haul most of the bricks for the courthouse. Cosby sold the wagon to Purnell Patrick, who used it on his farm until it fell to his son, Ben F. Patrick. Another interesting incident happened on May 11, 1889, when a heavy panel came crashing down from over the front door. Upon investigation it was found that the panel

Pitt County's Six Courthouses

This postcard view of the courthouse square from 1909 also shows the Masonic Temple on the left, which stood on the north side of Third Street and held an Opera House and the public library. Both buildings burned on February 24, 1910. After the fire, the brick shell of the Masonic Temple had to be dynamited and the debris was scattered on the city streets to fill the bad mud holes. *Courtesy of Judy Nobles Lewis.*

This postcard view, dated 1925, of the present Pitt County Courthouse shows the Pitt County Jail built in 1910 on the left and the Confederate monument erected in 1914. *Courtesy of Judy Nobles Lewis.*

had sat above the door for nearly thirty years and had never been nailed into position.

This fifth courthouse was damaged in a fire on February 16, 1896, when a firestorm burned most of downtown. The courthouse was saved with great effort, except the cupola on top of the courthouse, which burned. Thankfully, fireproof vaults had been constructed two weeks before the fire, which saved the deeds and the records of the clerk's office. The courthouse stood until it was entirely consumed by fire on February 24, 1910. The only record loss were the court papers of the clerk's office that were not in the vault. This massive fire also burned the jail, Masonic Temple and numerous businesses and houses. The county had very little insurance on the courthouse and jail.

After the fire, the county commissioners set about to build Pitt County's sixth and last courthouse. This courthouse was designed by the prolific architectural firm of Milburn and Heister of Baltimore, designers of eleven county courthouses in North Carolina. The Central Carolina Construction Company was the contractor with a contract price of $74,984. E.W. Foster superintended the work for the construction company and J.A. Case was the inspector for the county. The cornerstone, made of Georgia Creole marble and weighing 1,300 pounds, was laid on January 26, 1911, to a small gathering of people. In a copper box placed in the hollow of the cornerstone was material from the other courthouses, photographs, documents and newspapers. As the cornerstone was lowered into position several workmen dropped small coins under it for good luck. Pitt County is certainly lucky; it has one of the most handsome courthouses in North Carolina.

A History of the Town Common

Since 1970, Greenville citizens have enjoyed the large expanse of grass next to the Tar River, known as the Town Common. Frisbee players, sunbathers and concertgoers gather on ground that was once an overgrown slum, the "Red Light District" of town and one of the most historic sites in Greenville.

It was back in 1771 that a new town named Martinsborough was created on the lands of Richard Evans. Unfortunately, Richard Evans died before the town could be laid off and his widow Susanna Evans continued on with the creation of the town. On July 30, 1772, Susanna Evans sold the one hundred-acre town to Wyriott Ormond, Charles Forbes, Henry Ellis, George Evans and James Lanier, state-appointed commissioners for the town of Martinsborough. The name of Martinsborough was changed to "Greenesville" in 1787.

One hundred numbered lots were laid out on high ground stretching from a branch on the west of town in what was later called Skinners Ravine, along the river to what was called Town Creek on the east. The town common, which was available for all citizens of town to use for grazing their livestock, was all that overgrown land on the floodplain of the river north of what was called Front Street or later named First Street.

Little is known about what existed on the town common in the early years of Greenville's history, but there is evidence that a ferry, a warehouse and wharf existed on the waterfront as early as 1787. In 1791, Greenville became an inspection station for tobacco on the Tar River. From court records we know that in 1808 one Gideon Willis was building a 140-ton vessel named the *Carolina* on the waterfront. There was an old cypress tree on the river on the western boundary of town that marked the site known as Gallows Landing as early as 1835. On the hill above Gallows Landing (west of Pitt Street) was where Sheriff Benjamin N. Selby is said to have "hung many a man" and kept his jail with a huge key "over a foot long and weighing several pounds."

On the hill at what is now Pitt Street, three men were killed and twelve injured in July 1836 by the premature discharge of the town cannon. The cannon had been fired several times that day in honor of a Democratic victory. After the accident a party of men took the cannon and threw it over the hill into the river. The cannon was raised out of the river sometime later and after a long and checkered history, the restored cannon now sits proudly on the town common.

It was in 1836 that the first steamboat, the *Edmund D. McNair*, reached Greenville and started the Tar River's long romance with steamboats. The early town landing appears to have been at the foot of what was called Side Street or Short Street, the same place it exists today.

In 1850, the Greenville and Raleigh Plank Road Company was formed, connecting stagecoaches and freight wagons with a steamboat in Greenville. In 1852, the town commissioners sold land on the common to the Plank Road Company for a landing. The Company built a plank road from the river and after about ten years it fell into disrepair and the Company abandoned the landing and it reverted back to the town. The plank road went from the river to Evans Street, then down Evans Street to Fifth Street at Five Points, then diagonally west out of town to Wilson. This diagonal plank road out of town was named Dickinson Avenue in December 1889.

In 1855, the commissioners of Greenville sold land near the landing to George E.B. Singletary, who built a steam sawmill and brickyard on the property. This same property was later owned by J.J. Perkins in 1870, who built a steam cotton gin and sawmill there. In March 1878, Perkins sold his property to the Old Dominion Steamship Company and by the next year the Steamship Company had erected a warehouse, wharf and shed on the site. The Old Dominion Steamship Company introduced large steamers to this part of the Tar River and the area around the wharves on the river was described as having "thousands of bales of cotton" in season and a force of dozens of men. In 1877, the Styron-Clyde Line of steamboats had its own warehouse and wharf on the Greenville riverfront in competition with the Old Dominion Line. It was remembered that the hill was so steep leading to the landings that wheel blocks and chains had to be tied to the rear wheels of the wagons to prevent the heavy loads from running over the horses or mules. In wet weather, the drays would crash into ruts or mire almost down to their hubs in the mud. As early as 1883, the town planked the road leading to the landings, but with all the weight and activity the planks constantly had to be replaced.

In the 1880s, ice and oyster houses were built near the wharves by different businesses and local hangings were held before a crowd of thousands on temporary gallows erected just below the intersection of Evans and First Streets.

In 1892, after being flooded out by numerous spring freshets, the Old Dominion Line constructed a unique large two-story warehouse on their wharf with a platform leading to the upper floor. It was arranged so that during high water the lower floor could be opened for the water to pass through and the boats could discharge their cargo on the upper floor. In 1901, they also built a huge cotton platform, 84 feet by 136 feet, near their wharf that could hold eight hundred bales of cotton. In March 1904, a large flood put this new high-water warehouse and wharf underwater.

This rare view shows steamboat *R.L. Myers II* moored at the Old Dominion Steamship Company warehouse and wharf at Greenville during a freshet. Notice how they are still doing business on the second story. In 1902 a flood even covered the second floor. *Courtesy of North Carolina Archives.*

By 1900, the area along the river was a disreputable part of town. Known as the Tenderloin or Red Light district, it was home to some of the toughest people in town. The area around what is now the Greene Street Bridge and just below the intersection of Washington and First Streets was a trash dump.

By 1907, the steamboats were taken off the river. Gas boats, steam launches and oyster boats became the only vessels at the landing. The warehouses and wharves were taken down or left to decay. There were several efforts as late as 1921 to revive river traffic and build a municipal dock, but it was never realized. In 1909, M.G. Moye & Son erected a sawmill and shingle mill along the river at the foot of Greene Street. They leased the land on the town common between Pitt and Greene Streets along the river from the town for two dollars a year.

By the 1920s, the former town commons were covered in brush and numerous ramshackle houses. In the late 1920s, there was a small city park at the public landing known as Riverside Park. There was also a landmark known as the Tar River Oyster House that was built on Side Street. In 1951, the City operated a small park with a shelter on the commons between Evans and Cotanche Streets. In August 1959,

This postcard scene taken from the railroad bridge shows the view of the steel bridge crossing the Tar River from Pitt Street. The small steamboats on the right are moored to the foot of the Greenville Electric and Water Plant. *Courtesy of Judy Nobles Lewis.*

radio station WOOW began leasing land on the commons for their radio tower.

On December 18, 1958, the Redevelopment Commission was set up and adopted by ordinance by the City Council. In an effort known as the Shore Drive Redevelopment Project, they condemned the numerous slum dwellings (they had no toilets and rented for five dollars a week) and went to battle to have them removed. The Commission was able to relocate the people who had been living there to low-income housing. The land was cleared and a retaining wall and walkway was built.

In June 1970, the Greenville Redevelopment Commission, city officials and Housing and Urban Development (HUD) representatives from Atlanta joined a gathering of local citizens on the common to celebrate the restoration of the old town common.

Pitt County Places in 1921

Pitt County has always been predominately rural, but as the years have gone by, it has become more and more urban. Since "the country isn't the country anymore," the landmarks in what was the country have disappeared. Everyone once knew the name of the community they lived in, but now many of these places and names have been lost to obscurity.

There are other unusual and obscure places named in Pitt County in the records. In 1874, John S. Staton, one of Pitt County's state representatives, gave his address as Greysonville, Pitt County. There were also places called Chill and Prueston. A number of places went by different names at different times: Frog Level was called Glendale, Staton's Mill was called Ira, Fountain was called Reba, Belvoir was called Holland's, Oakley was known as Leens, Ayden was named Harriston, Bethel was called Brandon and Whitehurst's Station was known as Grindool. Over the years I have written articles about many of these communities and following is the history of a few more.

There was once a community known as Keelsville. Located northeast of Stokes near Oak Grove Church, this area was the seat of the Keel family. A post office was established at Keelsville on August 1, 1883, with W.D. Keel as postmaster. The post office closed on June 12, 1894, the mail being dispatched to Robersonville, Martin County. In December 1886, I.N. Keel and two black workers were digging marl from a pit on Keel's plantation when suddenly the side caved in, completely burying Mr. Keel. Both black men were badly hurt but escaped; however, Mr. Keel suffocated before being rescued. In early 1888, C.H.

PITT COUNTY PLACES IN 1921

The above image is of the "Yellow Hammer," one of the early cars of the East Carolina Railway. They were self-propelled gasoline passenger cars that were converted streetcars from Washington, D.C. The East Carolina Railway, begun in 1898 by Henry C. Bridgers, ran from Tarboro to Hookerton. The railway was sold to the Atlantic Coastline Railroad in 1934 and ceased operation in 1965. *Courtesy of Bob Newton.*

James taught at Mill Hill School, three miles from Keelsville. Later that year he taught at the academy in Keelsville called Oak Grove Academy and added a military department. On May 12, 1900, a post office was established at Keelsville known as Congleton with James R. Congleton Jr., as postmaster. It lasted until October 2, 1902, when mail was again dispatched to Robersonville, Martin County.

Toddy, formerly called Tugwell, located on Highway 258 between Fountain and Farmville, was once a bustling community with three or four stores, a depot and a mill. The history of Toddy goes back to Henry Clark Bridgers of Tarboro, North Carolina, creator and president of the East Carolina Railroad. He built his railroad through this community in 1901 with convict labor and paid for it out of his own pocket, with a little assistance from friends and relatives and a limited sale of stock. It was known by the locals as "Henry's Road." It was reported that Bridgers named Toddy for his best girl by adding a "Y," which caused a lot of opposition because it smacked at all the illicit liquor stores in the area. Bridgers converted old District of Columbia cable

This rare view of Calico Hill, Pitt County, taken about 1905, shows this vanished village formerly located on Highway 102 and off Highway 43 South near the Craven County line. This view shows the Noah Tyson Cox Store and the home of Horace Cox in the background. *Courtesy of Arleta Cox Wood.*

cars into gasoline-powered passenger cars and ran them on his line. The locals dubbed these contraptions "Yellow Hammers." In 1935, the Atlantic Coastline Railroad leased the East Carolina Railroad and ran it until they abandoned the line on November 16, 1965. A post office was established at Tugwell on May 14, 1902, with Milton H. Jackson as postmaster. The post office was discontinued on February 20, 1907.

Maupin was once a part of Pactolus and was chartered on March 4, 1905, when Pactolus was divided over the liquor issue. It was unlawful to manufacture or sell liquor in Maupin. According to its charter, Maupin's boundaries began at a forked holly on the north side of Grindle Creek, thence to the southeast corner of Satterthwaite's tool house, thence to a pine on the east side of the road leading to Tarboro, thence to the southwest corner of S.W. Williams's land to a persimmon tree on H.W. Hyman's land. The officers of the town were J.J. Satterthwaite as mayor and commissioners J.P. Fleming and B.B. Satterthwaite. The charter of Maupin was revoked by the state on February 25, 1911.

HAVE YOU EVER HEARD TALE OF…?

If people told you they used to grow silkworms here or that there was gold in Pitt County, would you believe them? Well, here are a few tales of the odd and the unusual in Pitt County.

Greenville Silk Company

The silk culture at one time was a large industry in the United States, being manufactured in North Carolina as early as 1826. By 1838 the demand for the Chinese mulberry tree (*Morus multicaulis*), the tree necessary to feed the silkworms, was so strong in North Carolina that fortunes were made from their sale. The mulberry trees were such an important commodity that the North Carolina legislature passed a bill to prevent the stealing of mulberry trees. In 1838 a silk company was formed in Raleigh and by February 1839 another one was formed in Pitt County. A joint stock company for the growth and manufacture of silk was organized in Greenville with Joseph W. Atkinson, president; James R. Hoyle, secretary; Dr. Robert H. Williams, treasurer; and Dr. John C. Gorham, John L. Foreman, Henry F. Harris, Archibald Parker and Henry Chamberlain, directors. The company had its cocoonery at Bensboro, along with a large grove of mulberry trees. By September 1839 they had purchased Gay's Patent Silk Machine and hired Miss Mary White to run it. The company turned out skeins of sewing silk described as equal if not superior to the best imported. In February 1840 they bought 102 ¾ acres on Reedy Branch from John Speirs to grow more mulberry trees. But by March 1841 the company went under because of debt, and the cocoonery and trees were sold off.

Distilleries and Beer Breweries

The manufacturing of alcohol was not unusual in early history. Pitt County, like all the other counties in North Carolina at the time, was not regulated as they are now concerning liquor. In the North Carolina List of Manufacturing for 1810, Pitt County had 727 stills, distilling 29,400 gallons of whiskey and brandy annually, valued then at $12,000. The making of homebrew continued until laws began to regulate its making and distribution.

It was in Greenville in June 1883 that M. Schwarz opened the Greenville Bottling Company, making and selling beer. Mr. Schwarz, in connection with Haskett, Smith and Bro., bottled fresh cold beer daily until one month later when Mr. Schwarz was bound over to New Bern Federal Court for violation of revenue laws. The Greenville Bottling Company was suspended and Mr. Schwarz left town. The next year in January 1884, J.H. Shelburn, in connection with a Mr. Anderson, opened a beer-bottling establishment, also named the Greenville Bottling Company. They advertised that they were prepared to furnish fresh beer daily: "Budweis, Bavaria, Staton Island, and Crystal Beer their specialty." The brewery did well in Greenville, since in 1885 there were fourteen barrooms in town. The Greenville Bottling Company continued into the early 1900s.

As for whiskey distilleries, in the 1890s there was a government distillery at Bells Ferry (Grifton) and one at Pactolus. In 1903, a number of people tried to get a distillery at Stokes, but that issue caused a small war there when those against it used dynamite to blow up the house of those who favored it. Later, the question of prohibition came up and when a state election was held in 1908, Prohibition was passed by a large majority and the state went dry on January 1, 1909.

Tobacco and Cigars

It is well known that the tobacco industry in Pitt County had its beginnings in the 1880s, but very few people have ever heard of Dr. Noah

Joyner's attempt to raise Persian tobacco in Pitt County. In 1851 Dr. Joyner, at his farm near Farmville, began to raise this tobacco, described as having a delicious flavor, for a short time, but nothing seems to have come of his venture. In 1886, Dr. J.T. Sledge, superintendent of public health in Pitt County, sold a local-made cigar called Greenville Future, the best five-cent cigar in town. It was a popular cigar and he reportedly sold five hundred of them a week. In 1897 the Winterville Cigar Company was organized with A.G. Cox, J.D. Cox, Dr. B.T. Cox, Josephus Cox and O.L. Joyner composing the company. They used Sumatra and Cuban leaf tobacco, with an output capacity of one thousand cigars per day. The company appears to have ended about 1910.

Iron, Gold and Silver

In June 1887, a black man dug up several gold nuggets on the farm of Grey Carson near Bethel. The gold was assayed to be the real thing and rumor had it that he had "a blue chest full of the precious metal as a result of many nights of hard and secret toil." Also in 1887 silver was discovered on the land of John B. Kilpatrick of Swift Creek Township. He found a considerable amount while cutting a ditch through his farm, which was pronounced by a chemist as superior silver ore. In 1889, W.E. Cox of Coxville found iron ore while cutting a ditch through his father's farm, more being found on a farm two miles away. J.B. Little also found a lot of iron ore on his plantation in Pactolus Township.

Holly Industry

Very few people know that holly used to be a very important export of the eastern North Carolina counties. In the early 1900s numerous people made money buying and shipping holly by train to provide Christmas greenery for New Yorkers, Philadelphians and Pittsburghers. One such company of men, consisting of C.A. Fair, R.H. Hunsucker, G.A. Kittrell and F.O. Cox, organized themselves in Winterville in November 1902. They shipped holly north, especially to New York, for a number of seasons.

Earthquakes in Pitt County

If someone told you Greenville was prone to earthquakes, you would probably think they were crazy. But the records reveal that Greenville has been hit by a number of tremors. As early as December 16, 1811, two earthquakes hit North Carolina and the shocks were felt from Richmond to Savannah. The second quake occurred at about 7:00 a.m., greatly alarming some of the state representatives by the shaking of the state capitol in Raleigh.

Another earthquake was felt in eastern North Carolina on February 7, 1812, which was described as a "strong rocking shock" lasting two minutes and followed later that evening by another shock of equal force.

The last known earthquake felt in Greenville occurred on May 31, 1897, at two o'clock in the afternoon. The shock rocked towns from Baltimore to Savannah. In Greenville, the only damage reported was loose debris being rocked around.

By far the most violent earthquake felt in Pitt County occurred at 10:54 p.m. on August 31, 1886, known as the Great Charleston Earthquake. This quake severely damaged Charleston, South Carolina, and was felt as far north as New York and west to Chicago. According to the local newspaper at the time, the fateful evening began fair with a slight haze in the western horizon. Suddenly without warning a shock wave hit, tottering houses and stores, rattling windows and sending loose objects to the floor. As the tremors continued many people rushed into the streets and bounded out of windows. The first tremor was said to have lasted only forty seconds, though to the participants it seemed much longer. It was described in feel and sound as "large pork barrels being rolled across a wooden floor." Ten or twelve minutes after the first shock, a second very slight aftershock was felt, followed in another ten minutes by a third almost as severe as the first. A fourth small aftershock was felt even later.

Reports of damage in Greenville and Pitt County ranged from shifted houses and damaged chimneys to store goods and dishes broken and scattered. The local newspaper told some of the comical incidents connected with the earthquake. A local merchant rushed out of his store yelling "Cyclone!" at the top of his lungs. Another merchant ran out of his front door as other men jumped out of windows nearly on top of him. One store clerk was sitting in his room on the second floor of a house reading when he felt the shock. He thought the house was going to fall so he sprang through a window to a tree and slid to the ground. A young boy alarmed by the shock jumped from a second story window and landed uninjured on a pile of bricks. Several townspeople grabbed their guns thinking somebody was trying to break into their houses, only to give up their houses to run into the street.

On October 22, another severe quake was felt in Greenville before three o'clock in the afternoon. The epicenter was again near Charleston, South Carolina.

Yonder She Comes Rounding the Point: A History of Steamboats on the Tar

One of the forgotten institutions along the coast before motor vehicles was the steamboat or freight line boat. The navigation of the Tar River has always been precarious, the water being too low to have easy passage most of the year. Before steamboats, local products like tar, turpentine, cotton and produce were carried down the river to Washington on long, flat-bottomed boats carrying two to four hundred barrels and drawing two to three feet of water. Parts of the products were bartered in Washington for northern or West India goods, but the greater part was shipped to northern ports like Norfolk, Baltimore and New York. In the golden era of the steamboat, Greenville wharves clamored with business. Large drays loaded with cotton, turpentine and rosin waited for unloading at the wharf of the Greenville Plank Road. The hill was so steep at the landing that chains had to be tied to the rear wheels of the drays to prevent the heavy loads from running over the mules. The following is a short history of the steamboats on the Tar and some of the events that mark their past.

The first steamer to plough the waters of the Tar and Pamlico Rivers was the side-wheel steamer *Edmund D. McNair*, built in Washington, North Carolina, in 1835 by William Tannahill and Benjamin A. Lavender. She was eighty feet long, twenty-three feet wide, five feet deep and about seventy tons burden. Her captain was a Swede named John Johnson and her engineer was named Baxley. Traveling about five miles an hour, with three tow boats, she made her first trip up the river to Greenville in mid-April 1836, and up to Tarboro by May. The McNair remained on the Tar River, principally towing rafts of lumber, until she was removed to the Cape Fear and Neuse Rivers in February 1839, going higher on both than any steamboat ever before. She continued to navigate the Neuse and Trent Rivers until she wrecked above Kinston, North Carolina, where her ribs could be seen at low water as late as 1880.

After her, Messers. Dibble and Bro., of New Bern, put three steamboats on the Tar River: the *Wayne*, the *North State* and the *William P. Graham* (called the *Governor Graham*). In April 1847, the *Wayne* was taken off the Neuse River and placed on the Tar River as an experiment. She made several trips to Tarboro, but was taken back to the Neuse in May 1847. The *Governor Graham* was launched in February 1847, was 125 feet long, 37 feet wide and had a 60 horsepower engine. The cooperative spirit on the river was lacking when the *Governor Graham* made its first trip up the river. She was refused passage up the Tar River by the owner of the Washington Toll Bridge named J. Bryan Grimes, later a famous Confederate general. The other three vessels ran on the Tar for a short time until taken off in March 1848 to run on the Neuse River. The *Governor Graham* was then removed to the Cape Fear River where she collided with the steamboat *Fanny Lutterloh* in 1854; the *Lutterloh* sank.

In 1848, a number of businessmen in Edgecombe County purchased a steamer in Baltimore, the *Oregon*, to run as a passenger and freight boat between Tarboro and Washington. It was the first vessel to use a new inlet cut by a hurricane in 1848, known as Oregon Inlet. The *Oregon* ran on the Tar and Roanoke Rivers until it failed early as a financial venture and was sold at public auction in Washington, North Carolina, on October 6, 1849. It was used later as a freight and excursion boat to Hyde County and Ocracoke.

In August 1849, John Myers and Sons, of Washington, put a little steamer on the river called the *Amidas*. Built in Hartford, Connecticut, it was chiefly employed in towing flats and carrying the mail everyday between Washington and Greenville. The *Amidas* began to lose money and she was replaced on the Tar in 1853 by the steamboat *Governor Morehead*. The *Governor Morehead* was built in Philadelphia for John Myers and Sons to make the Greenville run. She was one hundred feet long, twenty-three feet wide, iron hulled and fitted with a large salon for passengers. During the Civil War, the *Governor Morehead* was taken to Tarboro, North Carolina, and burned by the Confederates rather than have her taken by Union forces. The wreck of the *Governor Morehead* remained as a navigational hazard in the river below Tarboro until it was removed in November 1880.

In May 1855, a strange steamboat named the *Red Skull* was launched above Tarboro that could propel itself up the Tar River by the downward current of the river. When on its first run it lurched, jumped, worked for a short time and then sank, nearly drowning its occupants.

In 1856, the steamboat *Wilson* was launched and plied the river between Washington and Greenville with Jonathan Havens as captain. Havens once told an interesting story about going up the river in the steamboat *Wilson*. It seems one day when the steamer was off Boyd's Ferry, it received quite a jar on the starboard side. The exclamation of "Heavens, what a snake!" from the cook brought all the hands on deck. Captain Havens seized his navy gun, and after three well aimed shots, killed a huge moccasin, which was the size of a stovepipe and twelve feet long. Local residents said that they had seen the snake often and tradition had it that he had been known in that area for one hundred years. The *Wilson* was bought in 1859 by John Myers and Sons and sold off the river.

In September 1860 it was reported that a steam flat was being built at Williams' Landing, Pitt County, to run between Tarboro and Washington as a freight boat.

The next large steamboat on the Tar was the *Cotton Plant*, built in Philadelphia in 1860. It was a flat-bottomed sternwheeler owned by John Myers and Sons and later by the Old Dominion Steamship Company after 1872. The *Cotton Plant* was used in the Civil War as a troop transport and later as a tender for the *Ram Albemarle* in the battle of Plymouth in April 1864. It was captured by Union forces, loaded with cotton and sent to Norfolk, Virginia, as a prize. In 1866, it was sold by the U.S. government and brought back to run on the Tar, commanded first by Captain J.K. Hatton and later William B. Myers and George W. Howard. By 1874, the *Cotton Plant* had trouble getting up to Tarboro, so John Myers and Sons built an eighty-foot paddlewheel steam flat, called the *Pitt*, to run in connection with her to transport freight. The steam flat, the *Pitt*, was sold in June 1879 to W.O. Respass to run on the Neuse River. The steamboat *Cotton Plant* came to an end when she burned to her moorings at Tarboro on December 11, 1880. Her hull was taken downriver in February 1881 by her old commander, Captain W.B. Myers.

In October 1871, the Old Dominion Line put the large steamboat *Vesta* on the Tar River. The *Vesta*, built in Norfolk, Virginia, drew only eighteen inches of water and could carry three hundred bales of cotton. In 1872 they also added the steamboat *Isis*, which along with the

The steamboat *Tarboro*, built in 1880 in Washington, North Carolina, was proclaimed in the *Scientific American* magazine to be "the lightest draft hull afloat." Even with all her machinery and ballast, she only drew eight inches of water. She was sold off the river but eventually returned to make the trip up the river to Tarboro, North Carolina, for many more years. *Courtesy of North Carolina Archives.*

Vesta ran together with the *Cotton Plant* until 1874, creating a steamboat monopoly on the river, to the local merchants disdain.

In 1874, the Tar River Navigation Company formed in Edgecombe County and they purchased the steamboat *North East*, Captain R.P. Paddison, from the Cape Fear River, to get a regular line to Tarboro at a lower cost of freight. The Tar River Navigation Company dissolved in February 1875 after the Old Dominion Line ran them out of business. Captain Paddison purchased the *North East* himself and continued to run it unsuccessfully and he eventually took it back to the Cape Fear River in August 1875.

In 1876, Captain Alf W. Styron of Washington obtained guarantees from farmers along the Tar River, who were tired of the high freight charges of the Old Dominion Line, that they would ship a portion of their crops with him at moderate stipulated rates. Captain Styron started putting vessels on the Tar River like the steamboats *Edgecombe*,

Greenville, Tarboro, Beta and *Alpha*. He induced the Clyde Line of steamers to connect with him at Washington to carry goods north and west, which saved thousands of dollars to the farmers and merchants. The steamboat *Edgecombe* was built in Washington in 1877 by Captain A.W. Styron, as a passenger and freight boat on the Tarboro Line. The *Edgecombe* was a screw propeller steamboat and it weighed nearly fifty-three tons. In October 1877, the Styron Line launched the large steam barge *Harbringer*, to be run in conjunction with the *Edgecombe*, to remove ten thousand bales of cotton from along the river. Styron also built another large steam flat called the *Red Ram*. In December 1878, the *Edgecombe* had engine trouble about three miles above Greenville and a few passengers had to walk eight miles to get a wagon to take them to Tarboro. The *Edgecombe* was enlarged in 1879 when fifteen feet was added to the front, a saloon was added on the upper deck and the original cabin was turned into a freight room. She was sold by her owners in April 1880 to men in Washington to work the coastal trade of Hyde County. They lost the *Edgecombe* to debt and it was sold on July 6, 1884, to the Merchants and Farmers Transportation Company.

The steamboat *Greenville*, which was metamorphosed from the steam barge *Red Ram*, was launched in Washington in 1879 by A.W. Styron and is remembered as the most famous and beautiful steamboat on the Tar River. She was 115 feet long, 24 feet wide and only drew about 20 inches of water. Traveling about nine miles per hour, she was first commanded by Captain Macon Bonner and piloted by Arden Nelson, the oldest pilot on the river. She was later commanded by Captain M.S. Mayo. On September 17, 1880, while the *Greenville* was moored in Washington, it burned down to the lower deck from the explosion of a kerosene lamp. The *Greenville* was then repaired and enlarged. It had three elegant saloons, consisting of a ladies parlor, one main dining saloon and one saloon for black passengers. She was widely remembered for the delicious food served by her cook, Uncle John Cherry. The Tar River Transportation Company formed in Greenville in 1883 and they bought half interest in the steamboats *Greenville* and *Tarboro* of the Styron Line. The Tar River Transportation Company sold the *Greenville* at auction on May 19, 1893, to run on the Neuse River.

In September 1879, the Clyde Line put an unusual steamboat from Philadelphia, known as the *Defiance*, on the Tar River. This steamer was three-masted and schooner rigged and went between Tarboro and Washington. It continued to run on the Tar River until it was sold to the Norfolk and Southern Railroad in 1905 and finally dismantled in January 1908.

The steamboat *Tarboro*, also built by Captain A.W. Styron, was launched at Washington, North Carolina, on October 18, 1880. It was proclaimed to be the "lightest draft hull afloat"; even with her machinery and ballast, she only drew eight inches of water! Her design was even featured in *Scientific American*. She was later sold to businessmen in Swansboro, North Carolina, to run on the White Oak River. She apparently was brought back to the Tar River sometime later and was described in March 1912 as a slimy, battered and waterlogged hull moored to the Tarboro Landing.

The steamboat *Beta*, Captain A.W. Styron master, was launched in Washington in March 1887. Built for the Tarboro Line, she was a sixty-ton freight boat that drew only eighteen inches of water. On her second trip up the river in November 1887 she was burned with a load of cotton above Sparta, but only received slight damage. In 1888, the *Beta* was involved in one of Pitt County's gruesome murders. It seems William A. Parker, who confessed to killing General Bryan Grimes back in 1880, was taken from the Washington jail by unknown parties, lynched and hung from the Washington drawbridge over the Tar River. The steamboat *Beta*, going up the Tar the next foggy morning, blew its horn for the bridge keeper to open the draw. The keeper, seeing a rope dangling from the bridge, tried to pull it up but it was too heavy. He then stuck his lantern down and saw the body of a man, his feet just above the water. The lifeless body was cut down and fell on the deck of the steamboat *Beta*. Attached to the rope was a card, and on it in bold, clear writing were the words "Justice at Last." The *Beta* was sold later in 1888 and carried over to run on Contentnea Creek. The *Beta* was then bought in October 1889 by the Farmers Cooperative Mills of Shiloh, Edgecombe County, to transport cotton on the upper Tar River.

In 1887, the large steamboat *Alpha* was built by J.E. Clark of the Home Transportation Company to run as an excursion and freight boat. When it arrived in Tarboro for the first time in January 1888 it was a novelty to the populace, who were used to seeing low-decked steam flats. The steamboat had a tall mast pole and constantly ran into and tore up the telegraph lines that crossed the river. It was sold in June 1891 to run as an excursion boat to Ocracoke.

At the same time the Styron and Clyde Lines put steamboats on the Tar, the Old Dominion Line continued doing the same. In 1879, the

This photograph shows the steamboat *R.L. Myers II* moored somewhere along the Tar River waiting for the river to rise. She was built in 1885 to replace the *R.L. Myers I*, which burned. The *Myers* continued to run on the Tar River until it was sold to the Norfolk and Southern Railroad in 1905 and finally dismantled in January 1908. *Courtesy of North Carolina Archives.*

steamer *R.L. Myers I* was built in Washington by John Myers and Sons for the Old Dominion Line. She was a flat-bottomed screw propeller, commanded by Captain William A. Parvin, a local Civil War hero, making daily trips to Tarboro and Greenville. The *R.L. Myers I* was 109 feet long, 26 feet wide and drew only 18 inches of water. She was built first as a steam barge and later enlarged with three snug saloons, a main saloon 30 feet by 12 feet, a ladies saloon 12 feet by 8 feet and a saloon for black passengers 16 feet by 8 feet. She ploughed the river at 8 miles per hour and had a 400-cotton bale capacity. The steamer *R.L. Myers I* burned and John Myers and Sons built the *R.L. Myers II* in 1885. She was 200 feet long and the largest steamer on the Tar at the time. It continued to run on the Tar River until it was sold to the Norfolk and Southern Railroad in 1905 and finally dismantled in January 1908.

In July 1881, the light steamboat *Washington* was launched in Washington, North Carolina, by T.H. Myers for the Old Dominion Line. Commanded by Captain W.R. Myers, it could carry 350 bales of cotton. By late 1886, the Old Dominion Line built the steamboat *Beaufort*, which was exclusively run by Captain William A. Parvin. It was

The steamboat *Tar River* sits at the dock in Washington, North Carolina. She was built in 1886 for the Old Dominion Line to carry passengers and freight up the Tar River. In 1905 she was turned into a railroad barge for the Norfolk and Southern Railroad. *Courtesy of North Carolina Archives.*

This postcard view shows the steam launch *Eagle*, owned by Ola Forbes. Built in 1907 in Morehead City, it was sixty-five feet long and thirteen and a half feet wide. Forbes ran it as an excursion boat until it was sold to the U.S. government in 1909 to be used in the lifesaving service. *Courtesy of North Carolina Archives.*

taken off the Tar River to run on the Nansemond River in Virginia and around Norfolk, Virginia, until it returned in May 1891.

In November 1888, the Farmers Oil Mills at Shiloh and Tarboro chartered the steamboat *Cleopatra* from Elizabeth City, North Carolina, to transport seed and meal up and down the Tar River. The *Cleopatra* returned to Elizabeth City in February 1898 for the fishing season.

In June 1895, A.J. Gatlin started a new steamboat line on the Tar with the steamer *Carolina*, running freight and passengers to Greenville twice a week. In December 1895, the Shiloh Oil Mills Company of Edgecombe County launched the steamboat *Shiloh* to run between Shiloh and Washington. In 1896, the Old Dominion Line built the steamboat *Tar River* to carry freight and passengers. She was commanded by Captain William A. Parvin and was lighter and longer than the *R.L. Myers II*. The steamer *Tar River* was dismantled by January 1903 and its hull was sold in 1905 to become a Norfolk and Southern Railroad barge. In December 1897 the Old Dominion Line launched the steamboat *Edgecombe* to run between Tarboro and Washington. It was seventy feet long with two propellers and only drew two and a half feet when loaded. In 1898, the *Edgecombe* was cut in two and twenty-five feet was added to her length.

In March 1902, the Old Dominion Line withdrew its steamers from above Greenville and eventually removed all their large steamboats off the Tar River after they sold their boats and business to the Norfolk and Southern Railroad. Probably the last line steamboat appeared on October 1907, when the Tar River Transportation Company put the steamboat *May Belle*, Captain William A. Parvin, on the Greenville line.

The colorful and somewhat romantic age of the steamboat came to a close about 1910. Small steam yachts and oyster boats continued on the river until they too bowed out to better forms of transportation. The times of everyone rushing down to the wharves to see who was among the passengers and what cargo was onboard the steamboats have become a forgotten pleasure. The vanished steamboat is another broken link that binds us to the past.

Dr. B. Brown Williams Mesmerist and Clairvoyant

Dr. Benjamin Brown Williams, once one of America's foremost experts on the subject of "mental alchemy" or the relations existing between "mind and matter," was ranked as one of the most distinguished personages of his age. Very little is known about Dr. William's early life other that he was born about 1817 in Pitt County the son of William Williams and Susannah Brown. He attended some unknown medical college and began his medical practice in Greenville about 1842. It was said that in less than six months his practice equaled that of the most experienced physicians in the neighborhood.

Just before leaving college, Dr. Williams had seen a gentleman mesmerize a lady by taking hold of her hands, looking in her eyes and making a few passes from the head down with his hand. Although a skeptic on the subject of mesmerism, he was then convinced of its worth when the lady, while under mesmeric influence, told him what he was thinking and other personal things that only he himself knew.

According to articles on Dr. Williams, he had a mind too liberal to be confined to any particular "ism." He was determined to investigate all the different ideas in relation to the origin and cure of diseases; and for that purpose, attended lectures all over the country. The abnormal condition of the nervous system, produced by mesmerism, opened to Dr. Williams a whole new world of thought. He believed that mesmerism could help the recuperative powers of the body and he would use all the leisure he could snatch from his doctor's duties to study the subject.

After he had successfully practiced medicine for about three years, Dr. Williams gave it up and commenced giving public lectures on "magnetism, electro-psychology and mesmerism." In November 1847, Dr. Williams went to the Literary Institute at Chapel Hill, North Carolina, and gave a full course of lectures, submitting the results of his own personal experiments to the professors. After several weeks, the professors published a small letter in the Raleigh newspaper stating that after investigation, they believed in Dr. Williams's way of thinking and gave him a warm testimonial.

Dr. Williams began gaining notoriety for the innumerable cures he performed. In every city and town he visited, he left behind him many individuals restored to health after they had given up all hopes of recovery. In Fayetteville, North Carolina, a young woman was thrown from her horse and had injured her spine so badly that she couldn't walk. After fifteen months of pain, Dr. Williams worked with her for one week and restored her to perfect health.

In Cheraw, South Carolina, Dr. Williams's lectures on "electro-psychology" deeply affected a Dr. McLane, an old doctor of forty years practice, who after learning his principles, cured people of palsy and other diseases deemed incurable.

In Charleston, South Carolina, Dr. Williams's lectures and private classes drew many eminent people, among them being Reverend J. Boves Dods, the famous preacher from New York known as the foremost lecturer on animal magnetism in the United States. At the close of the course Dr. Dods put aside his former processes and theories and appointed a committee of three men who drew up a small letter for the Charlotte *Courier* newspaper of July 4, 1848, approving the soundness of Dr. Williams's teachings.

On the evening of November 28, 1849, Dr. Williams gave a lecture in Tarboro, North Carolina, on psychological electro-magnetism to a nice size crowd.

In the winter of 1849–50, Dr. Williams delivered twelve courses of lectures in Washington, D.C., where he incited so much interest on the subject of "electrical psychology" that many senators and representatives were members of his private classes. In November 1850, Dr. Williams lectured at New Bedford, Connecticut, where "mesmerism" was supposedly first presented to a public audience in the United States.

In December 1851, he went to New York City where after he lectured for a time drew crowds of over 1,200 people, filling every lecture hall he spoke in. He took rooms in Brooklyn, lecturing in New York City every Tuesday, Thursday and Saturday evenings. The other three evenings

Dr. B. Brown Williams, Mesmerist and Clairvoyant

This engraving taken from a daguerreotype that appeared in the Tarboro newspaper in 1852 is the only known image of Dr. Benjamin Brown Williams, the nationally known mesmerist. He gave lectures on medical hypnotherapy all over the East Coast, New England and England. His original ideas were adopted by other leading doctors of the time. *Courtesy of the author.*

he lectured in Brooklyn, and, every Monday he cured the poor for free at his rooms; on Wednesdays and Fridays, he cured those who could pay.

In July 1852, Dr. Williams began publishing a journal in New York entitled a *Journal of Organic and Medical Chemistry, Designed for the Student, the Physician and People.* It was a thirty-two page monthly, discussing properties of matter, food and diet, growth and physiology of plants and new scientific discoveries.

From available information Dr. Williams had planned a lecture tour to England in the fall of 1852. If he made the tour abroad, research has not turned up how successful his tour was.

Very little is known about Dr. Williams's later life. While a resident of Philadelphia, he married in Milford, Delaware, on July 27, 1857, to Mollie E. Anderson, eldest daughter of B.D. Anderson of Milford.

Dr. Williams was remembered as a strong religionist, being an able and successful defender of the Bible, which was to many a contrast to his scientific ideas. He was dignified, grave and earnest in his demeanor and rarely indulged in pleasantry. People found his humor dry, being a product of his presence of mind and disconcerted personality.

When and where Dr. B. Brown Williams died is unclear, being a project for later research; but he left behind him a legacy of original ideas that shaped modern medical hypnotherapy.

The Bridges Over the Tar River

Bridging the Tar River has been a long process in Pitt County's history. In the eighteenth century adequate means of transportation and travel was a problem. What roads there were in Pitt County were poor or merely paths and planters had a hard time getting their produce to the landings on the river or to the landing in Greenville.

It was in 1787 that the State Assembly established a free ferry over the Tar River at Greenville and allowed the county to tax the local residents for its maintenance. This ferry is described in the diary of William Attmore, who happened to be traveling through Greenville in November 1787, as a "small scow" (a flat-bottomed boat with square ends) and is believed to be the ferry that George Washington crossed when he came through Greenville on his southern tour in April 1791. The ferry landing is at the foot of what is now Washington Street, named for George Washington. The ferry remained in operation until sometime after 1823, when there was an effort to build a bridge.

On May 12, 1823, five commissioners (George Eason, John Mooring, Willie Brooks, John Norcott and Shadrack Shivers) advertised a proposal for building a bridge at Greenville. The bridge was to be of timber, with a length of about five hundred yards, four-fifths of which were to go through the low grounds on the north side of the river. The exact date when the bridge was completed is unknown, but it was finished by 1830. This first bridge sat on Pitt Street and the ferry sat on Washington Street.

The bridge doesn't appear in any known records until the Civil War. On October 9, 1862, a large Yankee naval expedition from Washington came up the river for the purpose of taking Greenville. The head of the expedition proceeded uptown under a flag of truce demanding the surrender of the town, to which the mayor complied. A small group of men then headed over to burn the bridge, but were fired on by a small force of Confederate soldiers hiding north of the river. One of the Confederate soldiers, W.C. Richardson, reportedly fired on the Yankee soldiers, killing one and wounding another. The Yankees pillaged Greenville and took ten local men hostage as security for their safe return to Washington.

On July 19, 1863, Brigadier General E.E. Potter, with several Yankee troops, came through Greenville while on a pillaging tour through eastern North Carolina. They raided all the stores and barrooms in town and burned the bridge across the Tar. Again the bridge disappears from the records and it is assumed that it was repaired or rebuilt at the same location after the Civil War. In June 1874, it was reported that a magician returning to Tarboro with a team of horses became frightened on their way out of Greenville. The horses ran down the hill to the bridge and one of the horse's breasts came against the railing of the drawbridge and a railing came loose and impaled them both.

In June 1879, the county had the old bridge torn down and a new bridge built at a cost of $3,400. It was said to have been nearly six hundred yards long and "the largest wooden bridge in North Carolina." While it was being worked on a free ferry was run in the daytime. The ferry contract was let out to Benjamin S. Atkinson for the unprecedented low bid of $19 a month.

In the 1880s the bridge had to be repaired often. The main problem was that the draw would become stuck when it was opened for passing steamboats and the people from the north side of the river would become stranded in town. In June 1888, the county commissioners hired J.S. Smith to superintend the major repairs to the bridge. The bridge was closed down for two months and while the work was in progress, a public ferry was kept from sunrise to sunset each day. The ferry was more of a nuisance than a help; it was necessarily slow, hard to get to and the road on the town side was bad. Often people had to wait a half-hour for their turn to cross and on occasion the water was so low that the flat couldn't reach shore on the town side, so people had to wade ashore or ford the river themselves. Soon after the bridge was reopened in September 1888, a large freshet came and vehicles couldn't reach the

The Bridges Over the Tar River

The old wooden bridge over the Tar River as it appeared before it was torn down in 1908. This bridge was popular in the 1890s for large bridge parties with music provided by Victor Reale's Italian Band and to watch the huge migration of eels up the Tar River every June and November. *Courtesy of Judy Nobles Lewis.*

bridge because the water covered the road through the lowlands on the north side of the river. Other problems included immense freshets that almost took the bridge away. Large ropes were tied to the bridge and to the trees on shore to save the bridge from washing away. The high water would also send large rafts of logs that had broken their moorings downstream to get lodged against the bridge. Men would have to cut away the logs so as to prevent damage to the bridge.

On September 3, 1889, the county commissioners, seeing that fast driving on the bridge was causing it damage, ordered signs on each end of the bridge saying, "All persons are hereby forbidden to drive or ride over this bridge faster than a walk under penalty of law." In 1889–90, the railroad reached Greenville and a trestle was built over the river near the Pitt Street Bridge. To cross the bridge thereafter was a constant danger, since passing trains frightened the horses, causing numerous runaway wagons.

In August 1899, workmen were working on the draw of the bridge when it suddenly came apart. J.T. Smith and his four workmen were hurled into the river, falling some twenty-five feet. Part of the draw fell

In this early postcard view, mules and carts traverse the first Steel Bridge over the Tar River on Pitt Street. Built in 1908, it was 18 feet wide, 1,556 feet long and had a turntable draw for boats. *Courtesy of Judy Nobles Lewis.*

after them, but fortunately they struck the water first and sank deep enough to keep the timbers from striking them. Four of the men rose to the surface, two swam to shore and the other two clung to floating timbers. One of the men drowned and his body was found two hours after the accident about a hundred yards from the bridge.

By 1907, it was decided Greenville needed a new steel drawbridge. In April 1908, the wooden bridge was closed and a steel bridge was built beside the old wooden bridge on Pitt Street. A ferry was run from the foot of Washington Street and a chain stretched across the river held the ferry in place. Three men using levers equipped with clamps moved the ferry across the river. They clamped their levers to the chain and walked the length of the boat thus moving it through the waters. As each man came to the end of the ferry he unclamped his lever and returned to the opposite end where he repeated his cycle.

The ferry is remembered as being a resort, especially on Sundays, when crowds kept the ferrymen busy. In 1908, an enterprising man conducted a cold drink and ice cream stand on the north side of the river, doing a big business and escaping both town taxes and ordinances. The ferry served until the steel bridge was completed on Pitt Street and the wooden one destroyed. The steel bridge, built at a cost of $75,000, served the county for twenty-three years, although it too was threatened several times with destruction by floodwaters.

In the 1920s the Highway Commission decided that a new bridge was needed and plans were made for a new steel bridge on Greene Street. Work began on the bridge in November 1927 and it was completed in early 1929 at a cost of $150,000. It was described at the time as being eight hundred feet long, twenty-four feet wide and having a four-foot walkway. It had a two hundred-foot fixed steel span thirty feet above the river. The new bridge was dedicated on April 27, 1929, to the World War I veterans of Pitt County. It is interesting to note that the plaques on the bridge state that it was dedicated on June 21, 1929. The difference in the date is due to the completion of the bridge ahead of schedule; knowing that they couldn't change the dates in time, they left them as they were (to confuse local historians). Upon the completion of the new bridge, the Pitt Street Bridge was dismantled.

Now with the new twin bridges over the Tar, the Veterans Bridge was dismantled in January 2002 and was eventually reconstructed across the branch known as "Town Creek" on the town common.

ECU FOUNDER'S DAY REMEMBERED

*In 1907 a little school began
Along the Tar River in North Carolina land
It grew and grew, it grew so big
It just had to expand
So I guess it's just about time
To become a university.*

And so begins a once popular song "It's Just About Time" or "ECU," composed in 1967 by East Carolina sophomore Howard Rollin. The song was written during East Carolina's struggle for separate university status and expressed the tremendous growth that the school has had since its inception.

It was back on March 8, 1907, that the General Assembly of North Carolina passed an act authorizing the establishment of a teachers college somewhere in eastern North Carolina. After a hard struggle with other towns bidding for the college, Pitt County and Greenville decided to float a bond issue of $100,000 and the college was awarded to this area.

There were four men whose efforts shaped East Carolina's growth and development in its beginning years. They were Senator James L. Fleming of Pitt County, who introduced the bill for the establishment of East Carolina; former Governor Thomas J. Jarvis, who put all his energy into all facets of the college; and William Henry Ragsdale, the superintendent of Pitt County schools, who was the largest promoter of a teachers school in eastern North Carolina. The last man was

William Haywood Dail, who at the fiftieth anniversary of the college dropped a monumental bombshell about the college and is certainly its unsung hero.

It seems that when towns were making bids for the college, the people of Greenville and Pitt County were not particularly interested in it. And when the bond issue came up, Mr. Dail was manning the ballot box in Greenville and chewed up all the negative votes. The bond passed with a great deal of opposition and resentment and Greenville won the teachers college.

And so, on the morning of July 2, 1908, former Governor Thomas J. Jarvis, chairman of the board of trustees, and a small number of others gathered in an old cotton field that would become ECU and with a shovel broke ground. As Jarvis began throwing the dirt, he said, "We have met here to begin the foundation for a great institution of learning that will be a power in eastern North Carolina…We never can begin to calculate the value it will be to North Carolina, especially to this eastern section, and more especially to Pitt County and Greenville." The ladies and gentlemen present then formed a semicircle around Mr. Jarvis as he stood with the shovel in hand and photographer R.T. Evans took a what-is-now-famous picture of ECU's beginning.

The very next week, on the afternoon of July 7, 1908, ex-Governor Jarvis, again in the presence of a number of people, laid the first brick to the new campus. The buildings were built rapidly and accepted by the trustees from the contractor on September 2, 1909, and the school opened its doors on October 5, 1909. On November 12, 1909, Dr. Robert H. Wright was installed as the first president of the school, which had a student population of only 172.

For years afterwards there were speeches made at assemblies and articles written remembering the beginnings of the college, but it wasn't until March 5, 1932, that a Founder's Day Celebration was held.

The ceremonies were sponsored by the Alumni Association, which recognized each of the chief founders and Dr. Robert H. Wright, the president for the first twenty-five years. Representatives of the first three classes to be graduated were introduced, as well as former members of the faculty and special guests. Also recognized were Miss Patty Dowell of Rock Hill, South Carolina, the first person to register at East Carolina and the first to graduate from this institution, and Miss Deanie Boone Haskett, the first person to receive a Master's degree from East Carolina. After the ceremonies, the Alumni Association sponsored a

This unique 1920s view shows the old Austin Building of the East Carolina Teachers School, which held all the administrative offices, classrooms and library. It was a focal point of the campus until it was torn down in 1968. Unbeknownst to most people, there was a secret government communications office on the third floor during the Cold War. *Courtesy of the North Carolina Collection, J.Y. Joyner Library, East Carolina University.*

This rare view taken in April 1918 shows the seventy-three senior girls of the East Carolina Teachers Training School calling at the Greenville Banking & Trust Company to buy liberty war bonds, purchased to benefit the Student Loan Fund of the school. During World War I, the Training School girls worked in the country and around campus to raise money to pay for liberty bonds and to give to the United War Works Campaign. *Courtesy of the author.*

luncheon, followed by a basketball game in the afternoon and a dance that evening.

From then on, Founder's Day was again made a gala occasion, but in 1934 the program was very simple, as plans were centered on a big pageant to be given at the twenty-fifth anniversary commencement. This, however, was not presented, as the death of President Wright cut short the plans. For a number of years, a date for a Homecoming Day for the alumni was set aside during the fall.

In the fall of 1939, Homecoming was held off until March 9, 1940, when a Founder's Day was held in order that Governor Clyde R. Hoey could dedicate the E.G. Flanagan Building in connection with the event. The Founder's Day of March 18, 1941, included the addition of a parade before the game, which has become one of the highlights of Homecoming Weekend.

ECTC (East Carolina Teachers College) didn't have a Homecoming or Founder's Day after 1941 until the spring of 1946 because most of the boys had gone to war. The Homecoming of May 4, 1946, was known as "Veterans Homecoming and May Day" to honor all the alumni of ECTC who had served in the armed services. From then on East Carolina has only celebrated Homecoming, and Founder's Day has disappeared as an event. With East Carolina's new growth and spirit, there are plans to revive Founder's Day as a celebration.

What the University has meant to Greenville and Pitt County would cover volumes in detailing. The influence of the faculty, officials and the programs brought to Greenville by the school has enriched the social life immeasurably. The students have mingled with the people, and the exchange of ideas on the whole has had a healthy effect on the community at large. It seems only right to remember the founders—"Ragsdale the dreamer, Jarvis the diplomat, Fleming the provider" and Dail the vote swallower.

Pitt County in the Movies

The following is a small compendium of the known films about or made in Pitt County and several actors from this area.

The first known film was a silent romance movie entitled *Stroke of Twelve* filmed entirely in Greenville. In July 1918, White's Theatre (now the Park Theatre) contracted with the Acme Film Company of Jacksonville, Florida, to make a movie romance here. Mr. Ben Strasser, the manager of the Acme Film Company, directed the film and Miss Brownie Brown, the Acme leading lady, trained local actors for their parts. The film began shooting on July 29, 1918, using the Pitt County Courthouse and Confederate monument as a backdrop. Some of the local talent appearing in the movie included Miss Nancy King, Howard (Tince) Hooker, Miss Bessie Ricks and an unnamed baby. The film arrived in Greenville from the studio on September 2 and played at White's Theatre on September 3–4, 1918, to packed audiences.

During the week of March 10–17, 1925, a movie was made of Greenville entitled *Who's Who in Greenville*. It showed the schools, businesses, streets, all the schoolchildren, as well as people on the streets during the week it was filmed. The film was made specifically for the "Who's Who Contest" sponsored by local businesses. The film showed the back of each businessman in front of his business with a number on his back. If you guessed the greatest number of men's names by the number on their back you would win first prize. The film was shown at White's Theatre from April 6–11, 1925.

In July 1927, a movie was made of the tobacco industry in Greenville and eastern North Carolina. M.Z. Moore, a Pitt County native who

Built in 1914, the State Theatre, originally White's Theatre, was the most popular theater in Greenville. The best shows from New York to the latest movies played here and brought the world to Greenville. William Jennings Bryan even spoke in this theater in 1918. *Courtesy of The Bicentennial Book; A Greenville Album.*

lived in Wilson, North Carolina, directed the film. The film covered the tobacco industry from the preparation of plant beds to the finished product, showing local farms and factories. The movie was reported to be completed in early September 1927 and to appear on the screen by October.

In late 1934, J.H. Rose, the superintendent of the Greenville schools, sponsored the making of a film showing all the schools, businesses, industries and civic groups in order to show off Greenville as a good place to live. The proceeds from the film were to be used to buy athletic equipment for the schools.

In June 1941, E.V. Atkinson, director and cinematographer for Reellife Motion Pictures of Indianapolis, came to Greenville to do a feature film of the city. The full-length color film called *Greenville on the Screen* included shots of city officials, city departments, industries, street scenes, churches, civic clubs, beauty spots and a large shot of Greenville mothers and their babies on the Sheppard Memorial Library lawn. Due to World War II, the film finally appeared in Greenville for the first time in November 1947 at the State Theatre.

In 1947, the Lord Warner Pictures, Inc. was organized in Greenville with William Lord as president and John W. Warner and Tom W. Foreman as vice-presidents. In November 1947, they made their first all commercial release, filmed entirely in Greenville with an all black cast. The movie, entitled *Pitch a Boogie Woogie*, had a mixed cast of local citizens and professionals, and contained a number of hit songs. The musical synchronization was by Charles Woods and his Rhythm Vets. The orchestra was from the A&T College in Greensboro, North Carolina, and most of the members were music teachers there. The cast included Tom Foreman, Herman Forbes, Esther Mae Porter, Joe Little and Beatrice Atkinson, all of Greenville. The movie first appeared at the State Theatre in November 1947 and again at the State and Plaza Theatres in January 1948. The movie was supposedly booked for theaters all over the country.

In early 1965, a team of moviemakers from Dominant Pictures in Charlotte came to Pitt County to shoot a few scenes for one of their pictures. Dominant Pictures, which specialized in B-movies such as *The Blood Feast* and *Moonshine Mountain*, used Pitt County back roads for some of their bootlegger chase scenes for their next movie.

In May 1969, The Roxy Theatre had a film made of the C.M. Eppes High School band entitled *Showtime At Half Time*.

Local Stars

In January 1939, Lath (Tarzan) Morris of Farmville, North Carolina, who divided his time between his two favorite jobs, buying tobacco and cheering for UNC-Chapel Hill at athletic events, landed himself a Hollywood contract. Lath attended the Rose Bowl game and persons listening to the game over the radio could recognize his voice. His cheering exhibition at the game attracted so much attention that he was given a contract to appear in a feature short film.

In 1945, Kathryn Youngblood, an exceptionally talented dancer from Greenville, appeared in a Warner Brothers picture *Night and Day*. Shortly after her movie appearance she appeared on the nationwide radio broadcast *Queen For A Day*. Kathryn Youngblood, a daughter of J.C. Youngblood, began her career by dancing. She first studied with Mrs. Carolyn (Hamric) Tolson and later with Mrs. Ramona Van Nortwick (who took her to California to dance for several months) and Mrs.

Marie Crate. Kathryn starred in many local shows and was featured in several Kiwanis Club Minstrel Shows. After she went to Hollywood, she was known as Kathryn Young. She worked for all the major studios and appeared in such movies as *Emperor Waltz*, with Bing Crosby and Joan Fontaine; *Escape Me Never* with Ida Lupino; *Fandango* with Yvonne DeCarlo and *Lover Come Back* with Lucille Ball. In the early 1990s she was still a well-known model and recognized for her beauty.

Dog Stars

In the early 1920s, Dr. John Humber, formerly of Greenville and later of San Francisco (a noted early cancer specialist) owned a handsome German shepherd named Clem, who appeared in several motion pictures and movie magazines. Dr. Humber was paid one hundred dollars a week by Los Angeles producers for the use of his dog until Clem died in January 1924.

In 1932, a movie star dog named Zandra, owned by Frank Barnes of Wilson, North Carolina, and later California, visited Greenville. Frank and his famous dog visited his sister Mrs. Julian White of Greenville, and thrilled people at the State Theatre and various schools in the county. Zandra appeared in several pictures, the most well known being *Wings in the Dark* starring Myrna Loy and Cary Grant. Frank Barnes owned two other movie dogs, Grey Shadow and Flame. Grey Shadow was famous for his movie roles in *The Invisible Man* and *Rio Rita*. He was the only dog in Hollywood with a bank account and made his own deposits. A Pathe Newsreel showed him buying a war bond in a California bank and the picture showed him carrying the bond to the lawn of his home, digging up his strong box, opening it and placing the war bond in it and then covering it up again.

In November 1946, Jean of Broadmor, a famous Collie dog who appeared in a number of Lassie films, was brought to Greenville to be bred with Bill Carroll's collie, Hallelujah Buzz. Jean, owned by a couple from South Carolina, was purchased from Kack Weatherwax of California, the owner of Lassie. The Carrolls's owned Carrolls's Sunny Lane Collie Kennel, seven miles from Greenville on the New Bern Highway. Both Jean and Buzz were shown onstage at the Pitt Theatre several times.

DR. DAVID RICHARD WALLACE
EMINENT PSYCHIATRIST OF TEXAS

One of the many Pitt countians who have struck out into the world and made a name for themselves was one David R. Wallace. David Richard Wallace was born on November 10, 1825, in Pitt County, twelve miles from Greenville, the fourth of five sons of Warren Wallace and his wife Phoebe Powell. Warren Wallace was the son of George S. Wallace (1761–1840), a Revolutionary War soldier from Pitt County.

David R. Wallace grew up on his father's small farm and went to school in Lenoir, Greene and Pitt Counties. David and one of his brothers, Warren Wallace, received their common school education at Miss Sallie Ann Jones School in the old Greenville Academy.

In 1846, David began attending Wake Forest College where he graduated in June 1850. In the records of the Wake Forest Baptist Church of August 1849 is found a curious note about Wallace, which says, "unanimously agreed to request Brother David R. Wallace to exercise his gifts before the Church." This is the usual practice before a person would get a license to preach. It is unknown if Wallace ever preached before this church or anywhere else.

After graduating from Wake Forest, Wallace began teaching school in Greenville and Warrenton, North Carolina. In 1852, Wallace returned to Wake Forest College and began studying for his Master's degree. He planned to be a lawyer, but on account of his weak lungs he changed his mind and entered the medical department of the University of New York. He graduated in the spring of 1854 and then took a short course of lectures at the Philadelphia Medical College, graduating from there in June 1854.

Wallace returned to Pitt County, where he practiced medicine for sixteen months. Once again because of his lungs, he wanted to move to a drier climate.

In 1855, Dr. Wallace moved to Texas and settled at Independence. While living there and practicing medicine there, he also taught Latin and Greek four hours a day at old Baylor University. In 1861, at the outbreak of the Civil War, Wallace enlisted in the Confederate Army as a surgeon of the Fifteenth Texas Infantry. The war stripped him of all of his property and he had to start all over again.

After the war, Wallace moved to Waco, Texas, and formed a co-partnership with Dr. J.H. Sears. Dr. Wallace practiced successfully until February 1874, when he was appointed by Governor Coke as the superintendent of the Texas State Insane Asylum at Austin, Texas. He served as head of the asylum until April 1880, when he returned to Waco and confined himself to nervous and mental disorders and was named as the first eminent psychiatrist of Texas and the Southwest.

Dr. Wallace helped organize the Texas State Medical Association and the Waco Medical Society, and was a member of numerous other medical societies. In February 1909, at the celebration of the seventy-fifth anniversary of the founding of Wake Forest College, Dr. David R. Wallace, at age eighty-four, was named as the oldest living graduate of the institution.

Dr. Wallace was married first in 1857 to Arabella Daniel (1840–1868) by whom he had three daughters. He married second to a younger sister of his first wife and had a son who died young.

Over the years, Dr. Wallace wrote small articles and sent them to the local Greenville newspaper. In December 1907, he wrote a long article telling how he passed the years and said of himself,

> *the world has been good to me, much better than I have been to it. Never was sued, never sued anyone; never owed a cent that I could not pay on demand. Have not and never had an enemy.*
> *"Far from the maddening crowd's ignoble strife; My sober wishes never learned to stray; Along the cool sequestered vale of life; I have kept the noiseless tenor of my way."* [from Thomas Gray's "Elegy Written in a Country Churchyard"]
> *Have never been seriously ill. Have been healthy and happy these many years. I have had all the happiness in life I could reasonably have expected. Have seen children and grandchildren grow up, settled in life, respected and doing well.*

While I still enjoy life as much as an octogenarian could expect, and gratified for its prolongation, I am aware I am a lingering guest at the feast, quite ready to go when the time comes, satisfied, with big-hearted, good old Bobbie Burns—"If there's another world, I'll live in bliss; if none, I've made the best of this."

Dr. David Richard Wallace, a man who led a fascinating and useful life, died November 21, 1911, and was buried in Oakwood Cemetery in Waco, Texas.

The Bomber That Flew Under the Bridge

Older residents surely remember that during the 1940s Greenville became a cherished "liberty town" for thousands of Marines, sailors and soldiers who were stationed at the numerous bases in the area. They came here, were entertained or entertained themselves at the Servicemen's Center, and made many friends among the people of the city. In 1943, a squadron of Marine pilots was stationed in Greenville and one of these pilots performed one of the most unique stunts ever recorded in Greenville's history.

At the outbreak of war in 1941, Greenville city officials became interested in getting the government to develop the airport for war purposes. In early 1942, the CAA (Civil Aeronautics Administration) approved the Greenville airport for the U.S. Navy as an auxiliary training base for the Marine Corps pilots. The Navy leased the airport from the city for one dollar a year and spent a million dollars developing it and enlarging its three runways. In October 1943, the work on the airfield was completed and on October 22, 1943, a contingent of marines arrived from Cherry Point, North Carolina, and took over the airport.

In December 1943, a squadron of Marine Corps pilots, VMSB-343, under the command of Major Walter E. Gregory, nicknamed "Gregory's Gorillas," was stationed in Greenville. J.H. Rose, superintendent of Greenville schools, extended the use of the old NYA (National Youth Administration) Center, now the site of the old Rose High School on Elm Street. The Marines cleaned it up and adapted it to their use. There were six to eight barracks, a mess hall and an administration building used as a squadron office. The officers and married personnel were housed in private homes throughout the city.

The men were trucked daily from the NYA Center to the airfield where they had daily flight training. They would practice takeoffs and landings as if they were on an aircraft carrier. The Marines erected a control tower, had an airplane maintenance section, munitions section, parachute section and a flight line of forty airplanes in a state of readiness.

These Marine pilots were well received in Greenville. Members were regularly invited to all the civic functions. The wives of Marines were entertained at teas and other social activities by the ladies of Greenville. All in all everyone got along in a great manner.

Most weekends found Greenville crammed with Marines and other servicemen looking to relax and be entertained. There were dances, scavenger hunts, dinners and bridge games at the USO at the Greenville Woman's Club. Besides dating local girls (which was a no-no for ECTC girls, but you know how that goes), the servicemen were at every sporting event. On Sundays after church, Greenville fathers would drive up and down the streets to invite several servicemen to Sunday dinner. Besides the local theaters, the servicemen were always in the Kares Restaurant and the Old Towne Inn. With so many men in town, it was said that the Vines House, the Salvation Army's Servicemen's Home (also called the "Buckingham Palace") on West Fifth Street, had every room and floor space covered in sleeping bodies.

In July 1944, Gregory's Gorillas completed their training and left by train to go to San Diego for deployment in the South Pacific. During their stay in Greenville, there were a number of incidents that created a stir. Military planes buzzed the college to the delight of the girls and buzzed the old Greenville High School to the outrage of J.H. Rose, the superintendent of schools. It was one of these Marine pilots, named Frank Lang, who pulled off the stunt of the century when he flew his dive-bomber under the Greene Street Bridge in 1943. I have to thank Greenville residents Garland (Buddy) Waters and Charles Dudley for information on this incident.

According to eyewitness Charles Dudley, Carlton Joyner and he were riding with Hallet Dudley in his 1941 Chevrolet going north on the bridge. "When we were about halfway across, I heard the sound of an aircraft and looked to my right and saw the aircraft coming and thought it was coming through the superstructure of the bridge. I will leave my excla-

The Bomber That Flew Under the Bridge

This postcard view shows the Greenville City Hall built in 1940 by WPA money at a cost of $134,975. The city hall and the fire station were both designed by the famous architect Frank W. Benton in the art deco style. The fire station was torn down in 1996. *Courtesy of Judy Nobles Lewis.*

mation to your imagination! When I looked back, I saw the aircraft come out the other side of the bridge and clear the railroad trestle. It is very hard to express the fear and excitement that all three of us had at that moment."

According to information, the aircraft was a Navy SBD, called the "Douglas Dauntless Dive Bomber." It had a wingspan of over forty-one feet and a long greenhouse-like cockpit with two machine guns at the back. Frank Lang, who is still living in Florida, has been telling the story of his daring feat for nearly sixty years.

A History of Bensboro

Bensboro, the ancestral home of the Atkinson family for 150 years, was located on the north side of the Tar River near Belvoir, Pitt County. The story of Bensboro begins with Benjamin Atkinson, the second master of Bensboro, who was a large planter and active merchant.

The best evidence of the importance of Bensboro as a center of business for upper Pitt County is found in the letters of John Gray Blount, a large commission merchant of Washington, North Carolina. Benjamin Atkinson shipped large amounts of goods (which included barrels of tar, pork, corn, tallow and peas) on large flats down the river to be shipped by Blount to different markets. Benjamin also operated a large country store at Bensboro landing, wherein he had a tavern from 1797 to 1802. In 1810, Benjamin petitioned the Pitt County Court to erect and keep a ferry at Bensboro. The court allowed it, but Robert Foreman objected to it since he ran a ferry near there already. The case went as far as the North Carolina Supreme Court in 1811, but Foreman's objections were dismissed.

Benjamin Atkinson died at Bensboro on February 2, 1816, age sixty-three years, and George A. and Peter Sugg qualified as the executors of his estate. On March 14, 1816, the executors sold a large amount of his goods at Bensboro, including a large assortment of dry goods, hardware of every description, one ton of bar iron, 300 bushels of salt, 175 barrels of pork, 50 barrels of tar, 70,000 pounds of bacon, 100 kegs of lard, corn, 20 barrels of brandy, 200 bushels of peas, wagons, horses, hogs, cattle, 70 head of sheep and more. This appears to be his store goods and perishable items, an example again of his large business dealings.

The next owner of Bensboro, Ben Ashley Atkinson, inherited his father's 1,500-acre plantation and continued extensive farming operations. Ben was also a Mason, being a member of Sharon Lodge in Greenville. A post office was established at Bensboro on July 17, 1826, with Ben Ashley Atkinson as postmaster. When Atkinson's health failed, the post office was moved in March 1838 to Falkland. In 1828, Ben was one of the men who kept books of subscription in Greenville for the Ocracoke Navigation Company. In February of 1839, the Greenville Silk Company was formed to grow and manufacture silk. The company had its cocoonery and a large growth of mulberry trees at Bensboro. In March 1846 the company went under because of debt and the cocoonery and trees were sold.

Ben Ashley Atkinson's wife, Rebecca Tunstall Atkinson, died at age twenty-seven on September 27, 1829. Ben Ashley Atkinson died at Bensboro on October 1, 1839, and his son, Peyton Ashley Atkinson, became the fourth master of Bensboro.

After Peyton finished college, he was married in Greene County on July 27, 1843, to Susan Virginia Streeter, said to be the wealthiest woman in ten counties and very popular with the men. By marrying Susan, Peyton increased his own wealth by managing his Bensboro plantation and her father's Streeter Plantation in the Lizzie section of Greene County.

Disaster came to Bensboro in early May 1847 when the old mansion house burned to the ground. The roof of the house caught fire from a spark from the chimney and since all the work hands were away in the fields, no one was there to fight the fire. The house and valuable furniture were valued from $8,000 to $10,000, a sizable sum at the time.

Peyton soon after rebuilt Bensboro into a place described as being of unequaled beauty. Bensboro was said to have been a large house with tall magnolia trees growing in boxwood gardens in the front and back of the house. Behind the house was a long line of outbuildings and slave cabins. Bensboro continued as the largest cotton plantation in the area and a small village grew up around it. An 1863 Confederate engineers map shows a church near the Bensboro plantation, of which nothing is known.

A large country store was operated at Bensboro for several years by Benjamin and Joseph W. Atkinson, until their co-partnership dissolved in January of 1833. The store was then conducted by John A. and Joseph W. Atkinson until September of 1836. The business was contin-

This tintype image is the only known photograph of the indomitable Susan Virginia Streeter Atkinson (1825–1895). Once the wealthy mistress of two plantations, the Civil War forced her to work to keep what little she had left. In a letter from 1892 she said she was nearly blind, almost prostrate from rheumatism and hobbled with a stick. She said she had a small garden of collards, red onions, garden peas and cabbage. In 1893, Susan and a granddaughter were almost killed when a strong wind blew down the kitchen at the Streeter Place. *Courtesy of Gay Bland Davenport.*

ued by John A. Atkinson until August of 1837 when he lost the store because of debts to Richard E. Rives and William Thigpen. The store goods were auctioned off on September 18, 1837. The goods included dry goods (silks, broadcloths, calicos, cashmeres), men's and boys' hats, saddles and bridles, gentlemen's and ladies' shoes, medicines, pots, plates, crockery, glassware, groceries, guns, tobacco, port and cotton. The store was soon after sold to Dr. John C. Gorham of Greenville, who offered the store for rent in March 1841. The store was described as then having extensive and commodious warehouses, a gin house, a cotton screw and two large smokehouses for saving bacon. Bensboro was a large pork producer and it was reported in 1843 that Littleberry Whitehead of Bensboro slaughtered a hog aged over two years that weighed 629 pounds net weight.

At the outbreak of the Civil War, tensions ran high and the question of secession tore apart the families of the area. In May of 1861 Peyton Atkinson was appointed a member and treasurer of the Disbursing and Safety Committee of Pitt County, the purpose of which was to raise and get money subscribed to help arm and feed the county. Local planters swore to the man to burn every bale of cotton to prevent the Yankees from getting it. Peyton set the example on the evening of March 17,

1862, when he torched four hundred bales of his cotton, sweeping away thousands of dollars in a few minutes. His example was followed by dozens of other planters in the area. Peyton's health failed and he died at Bensboro on February 2, 1863, of dyspepsia.

The fifth master of Bensboro was Peyton's son, Benjamin Streeter Atkinson, who continued the extensive farming operations at Bensboro. Benjamin was elected to the state legislature, being the first Democrat sent from Pitt County after the Civil War. Benjamin died at Bensboro on November 11, 1884, of pneumonia.

Susan Virginia Atkinson lived at Streeter Place after her husband's death in 1863. She is remembered as being very talkative and was an avid secessionist until her husband died, after which she became a Unionist and began telling everyone how much she detested war.

Many years later she is remembered to have passed between Bensboro and the Streeter Place in Greene County every two weeks. A black man would drive her in her carriage pulled by what was thought by the locals to be the finest pair of carriage horses in the world.

With the economic depression in the 1870s and 1880s, Bensboro fell into disrepair and the mansion burned in 1895. Susan died at Streeter Place on December 4, 1895. She represented the last vestige of what had been a time of gracious plantation living and a symbol of perseverance through the troubled times in which she lived. It is as if she died when Bensboro died.

Local Mineral Springs and Amuzu Park

Many years ago a popular pastime was traveling to resorts that had mineral springs, believing the water had medicinal and healthful properties. Pitt County possessed a few watering spots herself, and at the turn of the century they were the sites of large gatherings, dances, picnics and baseball games.

The most famous mineral spring in Pitt County was called St. Andrews Spring, located on Arden Nichols's place in Beaver Dam Township, about seven miles west of Greenville. It had grown in popularity and favor since 1885, when it was found to possess valuable mineral properties, though the spring had been used by the neighborhood for many years previous. St. Andrews was a very pleasant summer resort, especially on Sundays, when crowds of one hundred to three hundred people would bring basket picnic lunches and spend the afternoon.

In August of 1888, it was reported that a dance was held on a wooden platform in the grove at St. Andrews, the music provided by Marltown String Bandleader, Ulysses Joyner. There were hundreds of initials of the names of people who visited the spring carved into all the trees in the grove. Later there was a small hotel there made of boards, with a chimney formed from a hollow pine tree with a tin flue on top. A notice was seen posted on a pine tree near the spring. The sign read:

Come one come all
Come large come small
You are welcome to take
Some of the mineral shake.

Other mineral springs were located on J.B. Little's plantation in Pactolus Township in 1890 and one near Ayden called St. Abrams Spring. In 1911 Abram Cox, owner, proprietor and manager of St. Abrams Mineral Springs, erected a large dwelling house near the spring for the accommodation of the "lame, halt, sick, and ailing people." The local newspaper editor came to the conclusion it must be good water since in February 1911 he saw one man had sixty-nine gallons in jugs on his wagon coming from the spring.

Amuzu Park

By 1920, there was a movement to supply the need and provide a place for wholesome recreation and amusement in Greenville. In April of 1920, W.P. Clarke, A.T. Tripp and Claude D. Tunstall formed the Clarke-Tripp Amuzu Company to convert the Forbes Mill Pond, about three miles from downtown Greenville, into a pleasure resort. In May 1920, the Amuzu Park, with Claude Tunstall as manager, built a large dance pavilion, thirty-eight by sixty feet, with the upper portion devoted to dancing and the underneath housing numerous bathrooms for men and women. They installed a dynamo electric plant to carry 125 electric lights, a deep artesian well and a water system with a two thousand-gallon tank for showers. They built a 130 foot pier with electric lights out into the pond and stocked the pond with goggle-eye and speckled perch. They also rented nine steel rowboats for recreation.

The bed of the millpond was dragged and cleared of obstructions and a gravel bottom put in. Possessing a nice sand beach, the water depth went from two inches to twelve feet. They also had the grounds cleared of brush and nice gravel walks laid out all around in the trees, dotted with picnic tables. But in spite of all the planning and preparation, the park almost didn't become a reality.

In April 1920, the company offered season tickets to see if public sentiment would make the park a success. The beginning season price was ten dollars per man (plus war tax) and five dollars each for a woman (plus tax) and each child over six. Children under six were admitted free of charge. By May 8, 1920, they had sold only eleven tickets and the managers agreed that if by June 1 they had not sold enough tickets, they would refund all monies. Luckily, enough money was raised and the park opened on Monday, May 31, 1920.

When the park opened, they advertised that it would be open from 2:00 p.m. to 11:00 p.m. "during the dull summer days and hot summer nights." The Edmond's five-piece orchestra would play every Monday, Wednesday and Friday nights. A $2,000 Wurlitzer player piano would furnish music each afternoon and Tuesday, Thursday and Saturday nights. The dance pavilion was built "high and cool among the treetops, ideal for summertime dancing." It cost ten cents to get into the park, and to dance it cost men fifty cents on orchestra night and twenty-five cents on other nights. Ladies were always free. To swim it was twenty-five cents for men and ten cents for ladies and children; swimsuits could be rented for twenty-five cents extra. Mr. Ed Moye, with eight years of military experience, was in charge of the park and was the lifeguard and swimming instructor. In June 1920, a bus service was started, leaving the *Daily Reflector* office on the half hour and leaving the park on the hour, running between 12:30 p.m. to 11:00 p.m., with a fare of twenty-five cents each way.

On June 16, the park held its first square dance, the most popular of the dances held at the park. The sets were called by Leon Tyson and Zeber Tripp. The fiddlers were Will Forbes and Ed Moore, members of the Ye Olde Fiddlers Band. With its popularity, Thursday nights became square dance night. It is remembered that Rosser Laughinghouse and Tom Heath also called sets, and other fiddlers included Buck Moore, Tom Stokes and Levi Evans. Clogging was done between the sets by Ed Vail and Wyatt McGowan to the tunes "Turkey in the Straw," "Mississippi Sawyer" and "Arkansas Traveler."

In July, the park started having boxing and wrestling bouts every Tuesday night. They advertised "No objectional features or slugging. Ladies Free, men 25 cents and boys 10 cents. Bath tickets entitle each one to a bath that night."

The Amuzu Park had a successful first year and said they had forty-six picnic parties for church groups, Boy and Girl Scouts, business firms and reunions. The second year the park opened on April 29, 1921, and grew to be even more popular. Improvements at the park included new swings, a slide and cables in the trees for rope climbing. A huge water carnival was held on August 19, which included diving, canoe races and track events. Prizes were gold medals and season tickets to the park.

The park opened for its third year on May 1, 1922, but they began to have financial trouble. In May 1922, the Pitt County chapter of the Red Cross Life Saving Corps began using the Amuzu Park as a base to teach area swim instructors. After the end of the season the partners dissolved their co-partnership and in order to satisfy the partners and creditors, the Amuzu Park was sold at public auction in October 1922 to W.P. Clarke for $11, 300. The park consisted of the gristmill, twelve acres in the millpond and the thirty-two acres of woodland and park buildings.

On March 30, 1923, the newly formed Greenville Country Club purchased the Amuzu Park land and a part of the Gorman tract adjoining, giving the organization about 106 acres, including the beautiful lake and a rolling piece of ground on the Gorman tract. The Greenville Country Club kept the old Forbes mill and lake until the milldam was dynamited in 1927 and the pond drained.

Boston Napoleon Bonapart Boyd
Self-Made Man

Boston Napoleon Bonapart Boyd was a former slave who was born on Cotanche Street in Greenville in 1860 and worked as a paperhanger, sign painter and interior decorator. This description may not seem that unusual, but before his death in 1932, Boston taught himself to read and write by using the Bible, became a large landowner in Greenville and was the author of three books.

Boston was the son of Essex and Jennie Boyd, slaves of Abner Boyd. As was the custom at the time, slaves took the last names of their owners. In the preface of one of his books, Boyd wrote that when he was six years old his mother "offered me up to the Methodist Church for infant baptism to a colored missionary sent from the North to set up churches in the South for colored people, after Reconstruction. He put water on my head and said, 'God grant that you will be as great as Napoleon Bonaparte.'" Boston's mother vowed to raise him in righteous ways.

When Boston was thirteen, an illiterate freed slave, his mother "hired him out" to work on a farm for four dollars a month and board. Boston wrote "In 1875, I bought me a New Testament from a book agent for 75 cents." At that time he began to teach himself to read.

> As I could hear the people on the farm talking so much about God and His works—my mother, the landlord, and others—I began to see if I could find out about him.
> But to my surprise, about eight o'clock in the morning, alone in the field hilling potatoes, in the broad daylight all of a sudden I became overshadowed by a super-natural power…It was such a surprise…to me as to

Boston Napoleon Bonapart Boyd, Self-Made Man

This portrait of Boston Napoleon Bonapart Boyd appeared in the frontispiece of one of his three religious books he had published. Born a slave, Boyd later worked as a sign painter, paper hanger and an interior decorator. He served as a Greenville town councilman and accumulated thirty-six houses in Greenville, which he had all painted green. *Courtesy of the North Carolina Collection, J.Y. Joyner Library, East Carolina University.*

who could…tell God about a half-clad, ill-favored black boy as I was. Later on I joined the church and was baptized by immersion… I never used strong drink or profane language in all my life. I never craved it and neither did my mother allow it as she made that promise when I was first baptized.

Boston later taught a Sunday school class for thirty-four years, explaining and illustrating the Bible with colored chalk blackboard drawings.

Sometime about 1885, Boston married Mary Grimes, who was half Cherokee Indian and half black, from the Grimesland Plantation. They had eleven children; only four were living in 1968. One daughter, Dr. Alma E. Williams, was a practicing naturopath living in Philadelphia, and one son was institutionalized. Two daughters lived in Greenville, Mrs. Ellen Boyd Hussey and Miss Florence Boyd.

Mrs. Ellen Boyd Hussey, the eldest of the children, talked about her father in 1968. She said,

I started teaching in Pitt County for twenty-five dollars a month after making a high grade at a teacher's institute when I was seventeen years

> old. I had to sew flounces on the bottom of my dresses so I would look old enough. I remember seeing the kerosene lamp burning until late, night after night, in the early 1900s while my father worked on his writing. Even when he was working, hanging paper for seventy-five cents a day, he wore a vest with pockets so he could have his Bible to read and a notebook to jot down ideas during rest periods. He bought an old secondhand typewriter and I taught myself to use it and typed his manuscript for him. But he took it wearily from town to town before he found someone who would take his money and print it.

Boston was a strong advocate of equal rights for all people and he condemned the use of religion to teach white supremacy. His first book was *The Seventh Wonder of the World; Discoveries of the Twentieth Century, Natural Science*, published in 1903. His second book, published in 1905, was *Search-Light on the Bible with Natural Science; Discoveries of the Twentieth Century*. Boston's last book, published in 1924, was entitled *Searchlight on the Seventh Wonder; X-ray and Searchlight on the Bible with Natural Science, and Revised Searchlight on the Seventh Day Bible and X-ray, by Organic, Supernatural and Artificial Science; Discoveries of the Twentieth Century*. In the last book he rebuked Christianity in this country and remarked that "no race can hope to survive [when] all of its grievances have to be settled by other races who are opposed to them as equals, on account of color."

Mrs. Ellen Boyd Hussey said that he put her teaching money with his so that they could buy what they needed. Part he saved in an old iron safe in his house. Some he used to buy barren clay land and moved houses in from other areas. Boston acquired a farm and rented thirty-six houses in Greenville, in addition to his two-story home at 113 Reade Street. These houses, all painted green, were torn down in the Shore Drive Redevelopment about 1968.

Two weeks before he died, Boston bought two hundred acres of cleared land and seventy-five acres of virgin timber. This was during the lean depression years and he told his daughter Ellen that if things go worse that she was to move the family into the house on the land so they could raise food and burn the timber to keep warm. He also instructed her to let the tenants of his houses stay in them free, because they had no money.

Boston's daughter Florence, the youngest of the children, born thirty years after her sister Ellen, said her father "understood himself, life, and people. His belief was that if a man was honest and righteous, he would never be denied."

Floods, Freezes and Flying Objects

Since we have been experiencing unusual weather and a rash of meteor sightings lately, I thought I would give a little history of some of the odd weather and things in the sky in Pitt County's past.

From the old records we know that there were great floods, called freshets, of the Tar River in 1798, 1838, 1842 and 1867. There was a tremendous flood in November 1887 proclaimed to be the largest ever recorded in Greenville and two feet higher than the watermark of June 1867. The Tar River Bridge nearly floated away when one hundred yards of the north end was floating. The bridge was saved by a large number of strong ropes being tied to it and to trees on the shore. It was reported that the water even came up into the stores at Centre Bluff. The Great Flood of 1919 with a high water mark of twenty-four and a half feet was long remembered in Greenville.

The year of 1816 in North Carolina was known as the "Year Without a Summer." Snow, frost, cold rains and wind continued until June of that year. The farmers planted late, but the cold kept the seeds from sprouting. It was said that the birds froze to death in June and after frosts all summer long, it snowed in August. Very little corn matured and in many places in North Carolina the people almost starved to death. It was during the hard winter of 1857 that the Tar River froze over and people went back and forth over the ice. The next big snow occurred in the winter of 1876–77, when around Christmas snow fell to a depth of eighteen to twenty inches and remained on the ground until the middle of February. The next big blast of cold weather occurred in January 1886, when big blocks of ice floated down the river and lodged against the bridge. The blockaded ice became one solid uneven mass for a mile up the river. Also many townspeople went out to Forbes Mill Pond to ice skate. On February 11, 1889, snow fell to a depth of ten and a half inches. The low reached eleven degrees and three days later the temperature fell to two degrees below zero. In January 1893, the river froze over six inches thick. All the floating ice lodged up against the brick pillars of the railroad bridge and froze together for miles up the river. On February 17, 1896, a blizzard hit Greenville, leaving ten inches of snow with four-foot drifts. On February 18, 1902, snow fell twelve inches deep, the heaviest since 1876. The Tar River froze over again in 1917 and some people drove their cars on the ice.

In May 1901, an unusual occurrence of "black hail" was reported to have fallen. F.C. Harding said he had gathered up from W. Hartsfield's farm, below Ayden, a large number of black hailstones one and a half inches in diameter. He said where he found them the hail was nearly eighteen inches deep. A large hailstorm over Greenville in 1915 put eight inches of hail on the streets downtown.

As early as 1769 objects have been reported to be seen in the sky around Pitt County. It was during the tremendous hurricane of September 1769 that destroyed the New Bern waterfront that a large comet was reported crossing the sky amidst the storm. On the evening of January 3, 1857, a few people in Greenville reported seeing a large meteor cross the sky from northeast to southwest. The meteor made a shrill noise and left a long red tail that illuminated the sky for about ten minutes. Between September 2–4, 1859, an aurora borealis was seen from Tarboro to Greenville, illuminating the entire sky with variegated colors. It was said telegraph lines in the area were affected during the display.

In late February 1935, a meteor fell with a deafening crash in the woods on the farm of J.E. Jones, near St. John's Church, about seven miles southeast of Ayden. The meteor, weighing twenty-five pounds, was recovered the next morning. A large number of meteors fell in late 1934 around the Pitt County area. There are many tales of meteors crashing in the woods and fields between Farmville and Bruce, Pitt County.

In April 1894, J.A. Hyman reported that while riding along in the country after a hard rain, he picked up a large pike in the road. The fish was alive and had fallen in a small puddle and was flopping around.

On April 8, 1897, hundreds of people in Wilmington, North Carolina saw a UFO pass over the city. It came from over the ocean, moving west at a high rate of speed. It was described as an "airship," being circular in shape, with many colored lights and having a strong searchlight that scanned the city. In June 1897, S. S. Jackson of Littlefield, Pitt County, reported seeing a strange light in the sky early one morning before sunrise. Mr. Jackson got his wife up and watched the light move overhead in a small circle before it moved off. They believed it to be an "airship," like the ones seen all over the country in 1897. On April 11, 1950, several people reported seeing something mysterious pass over Greenville right before sunset. One of them said the "missile" passed over, very high, from the northeast, toward the west, and that its edges, or sides, were plainly visible during the dust storm that hit Greenville that afternoon. Several people at a gas station on Evans Street noticed the "flying saucer," or whatever it was. They said it moved slowly and that as it approached the sun, the saucer hovered in the upper right-hand corner of the sun and disappeared. On the clear evening of July 27, 1967, at about 12:30 a.m., an Atlantic Christian College student reported seeing an object in the sky near Farmville. The student was taking his date home to Farmville when, between Farmville and U.S. 264 bypass, they sighted an object about three hundred feet above the ground that "gave off an orange-yellow glow and was spinning." The couple was scared as they watched it hover, describing how they could see lights coming from inside and how it was as large as a house. The object supposedly had three levels, with lights coming from the upper level. They tried to follow it, but "all at once, it turned to the right, crossed the highway and was joined by three other objects." All the objects began moving away at an extremely high rate of speed and then disappeared. The Air Force at Seymour-Johnson Air Force base was contacted, but they reported no unidentified objects on their radar that evening.

Maybe a few people remember the UFO sightings all over North Carolina from 1973–75. There was one incident at the airport in Kinston and another over Goldsboro. On February 26 and 27, 1974, strange lights were reported over the Voice of America near Greenville. Later that year two highway patrolmen reported they saw more lights hovering over the towers. Somehow the local radio station got hold of it and reported it over the air. This sent a large number of locals and students rushing out to view the spectacle. They reported several floating lights over the towers and smaller lights floating up into the larger lights.

The Old Brick Store

Architectural history buffs and people who just like old buildings have enjoyed strolling down Evans Street looking at the old store facades. With the downtown coming alive again with the removal of the Evans Street Mall, there is renewed interest in what was Greenville's "Main Street."

It is here on Evans Street at what was the former Dapper Dan's that my story begins. Dapper Dan's was located in the old Greenville Banking and Trust Company and very few people know that behind the imposing classical revival façade of the bank lies the oldest brick store in Greenville.

It all began in January 1854 when George E.B. Singletary bought part of a lot on Evans Street (which was then part of the Plank Road to the river). In 1855, Singletary hired Moses Belcher from Farmville to superintend the building of the first brick store in Greenville. In 1858, Singletary mortgaged his brick store to William Grimes in whose family the store remained for many years.

Very little is known about George E.B. Singletary. In 1861, he formed the first military company to serve in the Civil War from Pitt County and was named as colonel of the company. Colonel Singletary was killed on June 5, 1862, in the battle of Tranter's Creek engagement with Yankee forces.

During the Civil War, the brick store was remembered as company quarters for Confederate soldiers. Many of the soldiers wrote their names on the walls and, while it was undergoing repairs in 1896, an article appeared in the local newspaper giving some of the inscriptions. The names on

The Old Brick Store

Mr. Tom Christman (left) and Sam Schultz stand proudly in front of Sam Schultz's Old Brick Store on Evans Street between Fourth and Fifth Streets about 1885. *Courtesy of* The Bicentennial Book; A Greenville Album.

the walls were "Sergt. Edward Lee 50th Va."; a name that could not be deciphered; "Hokes Div."; "Lt. Robert Snell"; "Jones of Flor. D. 57th"; and "Simon Glenn of Geo." Very little is known about who occupied the brick store building from the Civil War to 1875 when Samuel M. Schultz began a twenty-year stay in the brick store and made it a famous landmark.

Samuel M. Schultz was born in Richmond, Virginia, in 1855. After working in New York and for four years on a farm in Minnesota, Schultz came to live with relatives in Tarboro at the age of nineteen. He took a position with D. Lichtenstein, a wholesale grocer in Tarboro. He held that position for only six months when his talent for business so impressed his employer that Mr. Lichtenstein decided to open a branch store in Greenville and put Schultz in charge of it.

So in 1875, D. Lichtenstein opened a business in the only brick store in town. A few years later after new brick stores were built, Schultz styled his store the "Old Brick Store" by which name it became famous in Pitt and surrounding counties.

When Mr. Schultz came to Greenville in 1875, the motto of his business was "quick sales and small profit." He made such cuts in the price of groceries that he created a sensation at that time. People for miles around and in neighboring counties flocked to his store, recognizing him as the leader of low prices.

In early 1895, Mr. Schultz bought another store and moved out of the Old Brick Store in July 1895. In January 1896, the Old Brick Store had its façade and interior remodeled. It was described as having foot-worn stairs, folding shutters, heavy batten doors and dark winding stairs.

The next occupants of the Old Brick Store were J.S. Tunstall, a grocer, and H.A. Joyner, who had a dentist office upstairs. After the great fire of February 1896, J.S. Smith moved into the Old Brick Store and became partners with Tunstall. Henry T. King also moved his *King's Weekly* newspaper into the Old Brick Store for several months in 1896.

On May 4, 1899, another disastrous fire burned most of the downtown business district. This fire gutted the Old Brick Store leaving only the brick shell. In late May 1899, J.O. Proctor rebuilt the brick store using the old walls.

The "new" Old Brick Store continued to be rented out and was known as the Greene Building. In August 1904, J.A. Brady opened a grocery store in the building and P.B. Bowie moved his printing company upstairs.

Sometime later, the building was purchased by T.E. Hooker and remodeled again. In 1912, the store was purchased by the Greenville Banking and Trust Company and in 1913 they erected the handsome classical revival facade. While renovating the store into the bank, the original walls were exposed, which showed that the original structure had remained through every remodeling.

Remembering the Old Restaurants

As we make our sojourn through Greenville, there are landmarks and places we remember with great fondness. Some of these landmarks are the countless restaurants and drive-ins that have come and gone and remind us of our youth. Let us begin our rambling in the 1930s and remember some of these places.

In the 1930s, there were such restaurants as Club Pitt, Busy Bee Café, Carolina Grill, Silver Café, Dixie Gray Café, Red Gables Café and Smitty's Place. Club Pitt, also known as "Bloody Buckets" by the locals, was located at the intersection of Dickinson Avenue and Memorial Drive. It was a well-known place that sold oysters and had a weekly live radio broadcast. Ava Gardner (the future actress) worked at Club Pitt as a waitress. Smitty's Place, owned by L.A. Smith, was a popular drive-in on Dickinson Avenue, but it became Jones City Service Station by 1951. The Dixie Gray Café (509 Dickinson Avenue) was owned by Billy and Jack Whitley and was long a tradition in Greenville.

Probably the most popular restaurant on Dickinson Avenue was the Carolina Grill (located on the corner of Ninth and Dickinson) in the middle of the tobacco warehouse district, known locally as the "Dogshead section." The Carolina Grill was owned by George Saad, long an institution on Dickinson Avenue and the so-called "mayor of the Dogshead section."

Across the bridge on the left side was a service station called Chicken and Duke's Place that opened in August 1939 and sold gas, sandwiches and frozen drinks. Operated by Arthur (Duke) Andrews and Woodrow (Chicken) Andrews, they had curb service and played records. It, like other places along the river, was flooded out during the great flood in the early 1940s. Farther north on Greene Street were Respass's Barbecue Stand, Darwin Waters' Filling Station and Brady's Double N. It was in 1934 that V. Alton Respass opened a barbecue restaurant in a building formerly known as the Brown Derby. After Respass's Barbecue, the place became the Riverside Oyster Bar, then Crabby Sam's and then the Riverside Seafood and Oyster Bar.

A little farther north on the right side of Greene Street was Darwin Waters, called DW's, a service station that housed Sam and Dave's Grill, long a late-night hangout for the college crowd. The station burned and Sam and Dave's moved down the street. At the fork of Greene Street and the Pactolus Highway, Mr. and Mrs. Clarence L. Brady opened Brady's Double N Restaurant in 1947. It later reopened in July 1955 as The Flamingo, with Carlos O. Gardner as manager. This place is now long gone.

Coming back to downtown Greenville, there were various restaurants near Five Points in the 1940s such as the New Greenville Café, Kares Restaurant, Mary Ann Soda Shop, Dixie Grill, Mirror House, Victory Grill and the Olde Towne Inn.

Hulda E. Corey and her daughter Patsy Corey stand in front of the Mirror House Restaurant, located on the west side of Evans Street, south of Five Points. The building was built by Howard Bodkin in 1946 and the Mirror House closed in 1949 and became the Jimbo Williams Shoe Shop in 1950. *Courtesy of Patsy Corey Styron and Lindy Corey.*

Remembering the Old Restaurants

In 1938, Chris Kares bought Lauteres Candy Palace on Evans Street, a few doors north of Five Points, and opened Kares Restaurant. It lasted until the early 1960s.

The Dixie Grill was located between what is now BW's and Cubbies. In January 1944, I.R. Joseph opened the Victory Grill at Five Points. In November 1948, it was bought by Hassen Barakey who had been in business with George Saad in the Carolina Grill for a time.

After World War II, William M. Swindell opened the popular Mary Ann Soda Shop at Five Points. The Mary Ann remained open until 1965. The Map Party House and Pizza Parlor was located over the Mary Ann Soda Shop.

But certainly the most popular restaurant over the years was the Olde Towne Inn, located at 117 East Fifth Street in the old municipal building (where the former O'Rocks was). The Olde Towne Inn opened August 10, 1940, featured a singer and orchestra, and was the first air-conditioned restaurant in Greenville. During World War II, the restaurant had a room named the "Marine Room" in honor of the local troops stationed in the area. On April 22, 1942, the students of ECTC blacklisted and boycotted Olde Towne Inn when the restaurant put out circulars in the area military camps saying, "Come to Greenville, the city beautiful, 2,000 beautiful girls awaiting you with open arms, for real Southern hospitality, visit the Marine Room, at the Olde Towne Inn."

The Olde Towne Inn is remembered for its dinner special in 1960 when you could get one meat, two vegetables and a drink for eighty-eight cents. But then a bottle of Pepsi only cost seven cents. The Olde Towne Inn lasted until 1980.

Other restaurants in Greenville in the 1960s were the **Riggs House**, Cinderella, Ivory Castle Drive-In, El Patio Drive-In, Sidney's Drive-In, the Silo, the Candlewick Inn, Venters Grill, the Space House Restaurant and Dora's Tower Grill.

The Riggs House was a very popular all-night eatery located at 1201 Dickinson Avenue, next to the Carolina Gulf Station. It opened in August 1958 and served omelets, which were a new thing to most people in the area. It went out of business in the mid-1980s and the building was torn down in June 1987.

Dora's Tower Grill, known locally as Ma Dora's, was located on what is now Greenville Boulevard across from what is **Ragazzi's Restaurant**. It was named for the fire tower which stood nearby and was considered to be out in the middle of nowhere in the 1960s. Those eighteen years

This photograph shows Wilbur Hardee's popular Greenville restaurant known as the Silo #2 on Memorial Drive. It was operated here from 1963 to 1989. It was the former home of Dr. C. F. Keuzenkamp, a German chiropractor. *Courtesy of the North Carolina Collection, J.Y. Joyner Library, East Carolina University.*

This illustration shows the first Hardee's Drive-in Restaurant, which was opened on September 9, 1960, by Wilbur Hardee on Fourteenth Street in Greenville. Hardee sold off his Hardee's Restaurant chain to others that created Hardee's Food Systems in Rocky Mount and franchised it across the country. After serving as other businesses, the building was torn down in December 1999. *Courtesy of the author.*

of age and older went there for great hamburgers and beer. There was even a wooden dance floor outside. East Carolina blacklisted the place for coeds since they sold beer—but that didn't stop some from sneaking out there.

And so more restaurants and landmarks come and go in Greenville.

JESSE JAMES'S BROTHER AND THE TREASURE OF YANKEE HALL

There has been a long-held tradition told in Pitt County that there was a man from Pactolus whose daughter married Frank James, the outlaw, brother of Jesse James. The tale, first found written in 1890, has grown over the years to include stories of hidden treasure in the Pactolus area.

To understand the tradition we have to go back to the beginning of the story. It seems there was an Irishman named Sam Ralston (1778–1829) who located himself on the north side of the Tar River at a place called Yankee Hall, about one mile from Pactolus. Ralston was a wealthy merchant and shipbuilder and after his death his nephew, Sam Ralston, continued on with his mercantile business.

Sometime later Ralston, the nephew, got into a fight with a man named Cherry and killed him. Ralston fled the county before the law got hold of him and disappeared. It was said years later that he became a wealthy Santa Fe trader.

When Ralston fled, he left his two daughters under the care of his store clerk, Churchill Perkins. Perkins became their guardian and took care of their needs. Suddenly, about two years later, Mrs. Ralston and the two daughters disappeared mysteriously. It was said that they had gone to Missouri to join Mr. Ralston.

Years later in 1875, it was reported around the country that an "Anne Ralston" of Independence, Missouri, had run off and married Frank James, the outlaw. This was enough for the locals to believe she was one of the Ralstons of Yankee Hall.

In the 1940s, G.H. Little and J.J. Satterthwaite of Pactolus told the following related story. In 1895, Little and Satterthwaite were in business together and had a store at Pactolus. One day a stranger came into town who called himself John Thomas. He said he was from Falkland, on the other side of the county, and hired himself to the E.M. Short Lumber Company. The company was cutting and shipping logs down by the old Yankee Hall Landing, then known as Perkins Landing. Thomas lived at the logging camp and tended to the horses.

The locals found him peculiar; on one occasion when Mr. Short couldn't meet payroll at the sawmill, Thomas told his fellow workers he would pay them and get the money from Short later. It seemed odd that a logger should have several hundred dollars. Another odd thing was that he never received or sent any mail through the Pactolus post office. He would go off on the train, staying a day or two at a time, and say to others he had been for his mail.

Once Mr. Thomas became sick and stayed at the store of B.B. Satterthwaite. While recuperating, Thomas sat around the store and joined in the general conversation. One day the discussion concerned the news in the paper about Jesse James's horse. Mr. Thomas spoke up and said he knew Mrs. James very well, and Mr. Little asked him if he knew where she came from. Thomas said he had heard that she was from North Carolina. This is all that was said on the subject and no one could ever get him to talk about Mrs. James again.

On the weekends that Mr. Thomas stayed in the community, he was seen taking the sawmill tram road down to the river where he would walk up and down the riverbanks whistling.

One Christmas Eve night, several families were on their way back home, down by the river, and were passing between two old cemeteries. They looked down toward the river where the old Ralston house used to sit and saw a light moving around. They became frightened and ran the rest of the way home. By the next day the word had gotten out about the strange sighting.

Mr. Little and Mr. Satterthwaite went down to investigate the claim that someone had dug up a large walnut tree there. Sure enough, a walnut tree was dug up and the tree roots show that they had been growing around something square. There were tracks from a single person around the old Ralston house cellar ruins and upon investigating further, another hole was found dug in a cotton patch near the cellar. The small hole looked as if it had the imprint of a small store jar.

The next day, Mr. Thomas appeared at the store in Pactolus. He said, "good-bye," and remarked, "I'll not come this way again." He had quit his job. He got on the train and was never heard from again.

Mr. Little and Mr. Satterthwaite came up with the conclusion that Mr. Thomas was a surveyor and had been furnished a map by Mrs. James, showing where her father had buried money and planted a walnut tree over it.

SPANISH FLU EPIDEMIC OF 1918

While the allied armies of the First World War were only six weeks away from victory in the trenches of Europe, an unknown virus called the Spanish flu slayed hundreds of thousands of Americans in a few autumn weeks in 1918. The mysterious killer, which was far deadlier than any weapons of war and never identified by medical scientists of that day, killed by some estimates between twenty and fifty million people worldwide. And as suddenly as it appeared it disappeared.

The Spanish flu was so named because it was believed to have originated in Spain and because a similar epidemic had occurred in Spain and Europe in 1889–90. Some believed that the epidemic came from the Orient because the Germans mentioned the disease occurring along the eastern front in the summer and fall of 1917. Some investigators say the influenza came to America on a Scandinavian steamer that arrived at an Atlantic port with two hundred cases on board. Still others say it came into this country on a Coast Guard cutter returning from convoy duty. However it got here, it spread incredibly fast and over vast distances.

The first major outbreak apparently struck first at Camp Funston, Fort Riley, Kansas, in March of 1918. Through the spring and summer it did little damage. But when autumn came it returned with a vengeance. It ravaged army camps, cities and villages all over the nation. The flu began with a high fever and aching bones. Many cases developed into pneumonia after about three days. The lungs of victims would fill with fluid, causing death.

In North Carolina it appears that the Spanish flu was first misdiagnosed as typhoid fever. Nothing is found in the newspapers on the

This view shows the new courthouse in 1911, with the small brick Register of Deeds office on the far left. In the center is the H.C. Edwards Building constructed in 1911, with a theater upstairs and offices below. The building on the left is the Wiley P. Norcott Barber Shop and Billiard Hall, built in 1910. Because of the lack of a hospital the courthouse was used as an emergency hospital during the Spanish flu epidemic of 1918. *Courtesy of Libby Dudley Turner.*

subject, except the alarming growth rate of typhoid fever in the state. No alarm for precaution of the flu was given in the newspapers until late September 1918. By then it had already begun its ravages on the populace.

The first notice of the epidemic in Greenville occurred on October 5, 1918, when Mayor Albion Dunn made a proclamation in the interest of public health. By order of the city alderman, Mayor Dunn closed "all places of public assembly, including moving picture theaters, schools, churches, and Sunday schools" until the state of public health warranted the suspension of the order. On October 9, one of the few doctors in town told the local newspaper that there were at least 250 cases of the influenza in the city and at the East Carolina Teachers College. While most of the patients were getting along well and no deaths were reported, some were quite sick, among them being Charles S. Forbes, Hinton Best, H.L. Allen, Samuel T. White and S.G. Wilkerson.

Because people were still going about their business and basically ignoring the mayor's proclamation, Mayor Dunn as the secretary of the Pitt County Board of Health ordered everything closed by order of the Board of Health. This quarantine order included factories, warehouses, schools, churches, theaters and all places where crowds were accustomed to assemble. This order went into effect on October 9 and any violator would be fined fifty dollars or imprisoned for thirty days. All persons were requested not to congregate or gather on the streets or corners and that the sheriff, constables and officers were to rigidly enforce this order. The local newspaper complained that the order hadn't closed the courts, which were a dangerous breeding ground of flu and that the corners of Fourth and Evans and Five Points were still crowded with all classes of idlers.

By October 15, 1918, the Pitt County Board of Health announced its plans to combat the epidemic. Since most of the doctors in the county were off at war, each community had to take care of itself the best way it could. The executive board of the local Red Cross was expected to take charge in each township. Each township was to have several committees, including an intelligence committee, nursing committee, finance committee and transportation committee. The intelligence committee was to take a daily note of the needs of every patient and make a daily report to the local Red Cross chairman. The nursing committee was to list and distribute every available person who would be willing to care for the sick and to inform patients and their families of the most elementary preventatives and remedies. The finance committee was to list the names of persons willing to contribute money for necessary relief. The transportation committee was to get cars or some other conveyances to distribute food, nurses and other essentials to the patients. Each township organization was organized on October 16.

Because whole families were stricken and there was no hospital, on October 17 the Red Cross opened an emergency hospital in the county courthouse. The hospital opened with seven patients and the nurses the first night were Miss Maude Lee and Mrs. Marletta Dixon. On October 18, a soup kitchen was opened in the Greenville High School under the supervision of Miss Clara Carroll and Mrs. Travis Hooker, and assisted by the high school domestic science students. The first day they carried soup and broth to seventy black and white sufferers all over town.

By October 30, 1918, Dr. C.T. Fryer, Pitt County health officer, reported the flu in Greenville was on the wane, but the county was reported to still have a number of serious cases. It is remembered that people needing help in the country would put a cloth on their mailbox and the mailman knew that the family needed help and would notify someone. How many all told in Pitt County died from the flu is unknown, but looking at the death certificates it appears the number could reach three hundred. The quarantine was lifted on November 5, 1918, with the opening of the Tobacco Market. The influenza had paralyzed businesses and set back all kinds of enterprises. But it left as quickly as it came.

The Spanish flu struck every country in the world, sparing only the island of St. Helena and Mauritius Island in the Indian Ocean. India's death toll was more than 1.5 million. The Dutch West Indies was nearly a million and the United States had nearly 600,000. The continent of North America suffered a death toll of nearly 1.1 million. It is unknown what the death toll was in Europe, Russia and China. And where it went remains a medical mystery.

In 1951, a medical team led by Dr. Albert P. McKee of Iowa State University journeyed to Alaska. There they exhumed the bodies of several flu victims preserved in the frozen tundra. Lung sections were packed in ice and sent back to Iowa City in an effort to recover the virus and infect laboratory animals. But the virus could not be recovered, thus blocking efforts to isolate and identify it and possibly prevent another visitation. The outbreak of the Asian flu epidemic or "Hong Kong Flu" in 1968–69 may be remembered as not being as deadly as the Spanish flu epidemic, but it too affected people worldwide.

Dr. George Hatem, Legendary Figure in China's Public Health

Born in 1910 in Buffalo, New York, Shafeek "George" Hatem was a son of Mr. and Mrs. Naoum Hatem, poor Lebanese immigrants. Naoum brought his family to Greenville sometime in the teens and opened a men's clothing store on Dickinson Avenue. During the Depression, Naoum moved his family to Roanoke Rapids, North Carolina, and operated a store there.

George Hatem came as a child with his family to Greenville where he graduated from high school in 1927. Hatem finished his premedical studies at UNC-Chapel Hill, where he ran track and organized the school's first fencing team. He then went back to Lebanon, and after doing his clinical training at the American University in Beirut, he graduated from medical school at the University of Geneva in 1932. This was in the midst of the Depression and he heard that doctors in New York City had to drive milk trucks to earn a living. So instead of coming home, he began traveling with the writer Edgar Snow until he reached Shanghai, China, in 1933.

Although he prospered in Shanghai, caring mostly for people with venereal disease, he began to think that any efforts to attack the disease at its sociological roots might be in vain. Mr. Snow wrote later that Dr. Hatem once said, "I didn't spend my old man's money learning to become a V.D. quack for a gangster society. Maybe these people up north (communists) are interested in putting an end to the whole business." In 1936, Hatem went with the writer Edgar Snow to Yenan, a Communist stronghold in northern China. There he became acquainted with Mao Tse-tung, who led the Communist takeover of China.

After the Communist takeover in 1949, Mao Tse-tung instructed Dr. Hatem to create the Army Medical School. This was China's first public health effort and it included a campaign against cholera and venereal disease waged with lay citizen "barefoot doctors" trained for nine months and sent out to treat millions of patients. As a physician, Hatem treated Mao Tse-tung, Zhou Enlai and many other Communist leaders. After the liberation in 1949, Hatem moved to Beijing to serve as an advisor to the newly created Ministry of Public Health. One of his first achievements was to close the 224 brothels there in a single day and treat all the prostitutes for venereal disease. During China's Cultural Revolution, Dr. Hatem was denounced as a "bourgeois lackey" and for a time wasn't allowed to practice medicine. In 1964, China was declared free of venereal disease, though it had returned by 1980.

Dr. Hatem, known to the Chinese as "Dr. Ma Haide" or "Virtue from Overseas," became a citizen of China in 1949 and married Zhou Sufci, a former child actress and later a leading film director. He became venerated by the Chinese for his dedication and was later honored by the Chinese for his services to the nation. Dr. Hatem was also recognized by other nations, including the United States. In 1986, Hatem received the prestigious Albert Lasker Public Service Award in recognition of his work during the Mao Regime, which was compared in importance "to the eradication of yellow fever and bubonic plague."

In 1978, Dr. Hatem returned to North Carolina for his first visit in forty-six years. During his visit to Greenville, he and his wife were honored with a special dinner by his 1927 Greenville High School class. He also returned to Greenville in the summers of 1986, 1987 and 1988.

About 1986, Dr. Hatem began another campaign in Beijing, China, to cure the two hundred thousand people suffering from leprosy. He established the Chinese Leprosy Foundation and gratefully received some assistance from his friends in Greenville and elsewhere. He is remembered as being horrified to see Chinese doctors covering themselves from head to toe to treat lepers. When he saw them, he grew angry and demanded them to change into their normal clothes. His willingness to treat and touch his patients, many of whom would cry because they had not felt another human being's touch in years, was Hatem's legacy of kindness. At the age of seventy-eight, Dr. Hatem, who made China his home for fifty-five years, died in a Beijing hospital on October 2, 1988. He died after having suffered from inflammation of the pancreas and a ten-year battle with cancer.

Dr. George Hatem is remembered with great fondness. He was described as "a happy and upbeat" person, with a great sense of humor. He was a proud father of two children and devoted grandfather of four grandchildren, who would publish a booklet of photographs of his family, grandchildren and friends to send each Christmas to his friends worldwide. After Dr. Hatem won the Lasker Award, fifteen publishers were eager to commission a book on him. All the offers and various propositions were sent to him by *Parade* magazine. Several weeks later he responded from China with a brief note: "Too busy treating the sick to toot my horn."

Tales of the Odd and Unusual

Mad Pig

A pig ran wild in Greenville in the 1930s and caused a whole mess of trouble. It seems that a farmer was passing through town with a truck full of pigs on the way to his farm in Bethel. He stopped for a drink at a filling station across the river and while he was pulling in a pig crate fell off the truck. The crate broke open and the pig scrambled out. The pig was evidently hit on the head pretty badly because it started chasing an old man that happened to be walking by the highway. The pig bit the old man on the calf of his leg and would have done more damage if the man hadn't gotten up on top of a gas pump. Surprised by it all, the farmer grabbed a stick and commenced to beat the ground, trying to scare off the pig. While this was going on, the old man was bleeding badly and the filling station man called the hospital. The pig then galloped off and took a large bite out of a passing motorist who had gotten out of his car to watch. The farmer ran up again and distracted the pig's attention by beating the ground with his stick while the motorist's family helped him back into the car. Making a lot of squealing noises, the pig then attacked the farmer. The farmer threw down his stick and ran only to stumble over a pile of used tires and sprain his back. The pig bit off three of his fingers. By this time the ambulance arrived to get the first victim, and a storeowner in the vicinity had come to the scene with a rifle. He kept telling people to get out of the way so he could shoot the mad pig. The man's gun failed to fire and he took a vicious swing at the pig with the gunstock and hit a woman who happened to be running by in the forehead. The pig bit the storeowner on the leg and scrambled off down a dirt road, screaming and squealing. The police were called in and one or two highway patrolmen showed up on the scene. They combed the area but were unable to find the pig. The hospital was busy that day!

The Ultimate Family Photo Session

In October 1897, Louis Flake came to Greenville bringing along his wife and eight children and while in town had their pictures taken. He had 17 taken of himself, wife and each of his children, making 170 photos. He then had 17 taken of himself and his wife together, making a total of 187 pictures all told. He said later he would have a few more taken after a while.

Ancient Roman Coin

In 1979, the local newspaper carried a story that seemed to come straight out of Charles Fort's *Book of the Damned*. It seems that a local man, James O. Bond Sr. picked up a cluster of marl long the North Carolina coast sometime in 1973. He noticed something foreign in the cluster; thinking perhaps that it was an old nail, he started to toss it away, but for some reason he kept it. Sometime later, Bond broke open the cluster and found an old copper coin inside. Bond, being a coin collector, looked through reference books, talked to friends and did research at the ECU Library, but could not identify it. He put the issue aside for some years but his friends eventually urged him to try to find out more on the old coin. So in 1979, Bond took color photographs of the coin and sent them to the Smithsonian. The Smithsonian sent him a letter back informing him that indeed it was an ancient coin. The copper coin bore the likeness of Claudius I, Roman Emperor from AD 41 to 54. So, how did a Roman coin wash up on North Carolina's coast?

General Cornwallis's Horse

In the eighteenth and nineteenth centuries, breeding thoroughbred horses was a lucrative business. Very detailed pedigrees and studbooks were kept, each reading like the Old Testament with innumerable "begats." One interesting pedigree that involved Pitt County concerned the thoroughbred horse Muckle John, owned by William G. Bullock of Edgecombe County, North Carolina, in 1839. Muckle John was a descendant of Hall's Union, a bay horse with a light mane and tail. Hall's Union was taken in Maryland during the Revolutionary War by the British officer Colonel Tarleton and brought to York County, Virginia. Colonel Tarleton afterwards let General Lord Cornwallis have him and he brought him to North Carolina, and after a time exchanged him for several fine geldings. Hall's Union begat some of the very best horse flesh in the state at the time. He covered several seasons and died in Pitt County at a very advanced age, sometime after 1823.

Graveyard Stint

On the evening of August 20, 1959, three boys were dumping trash from the local drive-in at the city dump behind Greenwood Cemetery. Two of the boys scared the other kid about haunts and ghosts in the cemetery. The young kid was so upset that his family brought a complaint against the other boys. The boys were brought to court for scaring the other youth and Judge Charles Whedbee sentenced the two boys to an hour's stay at midnight in the spooky Cherry Hill Cemetery for disorderly conduct. When the youths reported to the police station on the appointed night to be escorted by the officers to the graveyard, Judge Whedbee commuted their sentence. The judge thought the boys had suffered enough thinking about the graveyard during the week and didn't want to see anyone hurt.

Famous Midgets

Very few people know that among the large number of famous people who have visited Greenville in its past was P.T. Barnum's famous midget, General Tom Thumb. In April 1845, the celebrated man, advertised as being "twenty years old, twenty-seven inches high and twenty-five pounds in weight," visited first in Tarboro and later in Greenville and Washington. Another well known midget, Johnny Morris Jr., nationally known for the saying "Call for Philip Morris" and goodwill traveling ambassador for Philip Morris cigarettes, visited Greenville on May 4, 1948, in his "diminutive auto." He was described as having a pleasing personality and was a clever conversationalist.

Local Remedies

In March 1891, it was reported that a young man in Beaver Dam Township would tie lead to his horse's tail because the animal had a fondness for holding his "caudal appendage' somewhat one-sided. In July 1894, it was reported that Wiley Thomas of Carolina Township had some sick pigs and it was recommended to him to put tar on them. He used the tar a little too freely and after hearing a commotion in the pigpen later, he found the pigs all stuck together and one pig stuck to the side of the barn.

It's a Job

It was during Homecoming weekend in 1955 that East Carolina campus police Chief Jimmy L. Harrell was confronted with the most unusual case of his career. While making his regular dormitory rounds, Chief Harrell discovered a 2,500-pound mule blocking the first floor hallway of Slay Hall. Harrell recognized the mule as one of a pair of mules that had been brought to campus by a local fraternity to pull a hearse in the Homecoming parade. After the parade, the fraternity brothers tied the mules to a tree behind the maintenance building and left them there while they went to the Homecoming football game.

Chief Harrell backed the mule down the hallway and out the front of the building. When he tied the mule behind the building he found the other mule was also missing. He returned to the dorm and searched the first floor. No mule. Then he climbed the stairs to the second floor where he found the missing mule. It took approximately an hour to back the mule down two flights of stairs and out of the dorm.

In 1961, when Jones Hall was built, Chief Harrell was summoned to that dormitory one Sunday morning to remove a pig from a second floor bathroom. When Harrell got there he found a boy on his hands and knees scrubbing a pig in the shower. The boy ran out and left the pig in the bathroom. Harrell took the pig home and advertised for its owner to come and get it, but no ever claimed it. Harrell added that about a month later he had a great barbecue.

THE IMPERIAL TOBACCO COMPANY

Anyone looking west over the Greenville skyline will see the large smokestack and water tower looming over that part of the city known as "Tobacco Town." These architectural features belong to the large three-story plant of the former Imperial Tobacco Company of Great Britain and Ireland, Ltd. The Imperial was once the largest buyer of tobacco on the Greenville market for the export trade. The company left Greenville in 1978 and the mammoth building which covers two city blocks now sits waiting for someone with vision to see its powerful potential to Greenville's future.

The story begins with James B. Duke of Durham, North Carolina, who tried to take over the tobacco markets of the world. In 1890, Duke merged the five largest tobacco companies in America to create the American Tobacco Company. After having a monopoly on the American market, Duke went to England in 1901 and tried to take over the British tobacco market. In response to this, thirteen English family-run tobacco companies formed together in December 1901 to create the Imperial Tobacco Company of Great Britain and Ireland, Ltd.

In April 1902, it was announced that the Imperial Tobacco Company had entered North Carolina to start the tobacco war on Duke's home territory. The representatives of the Imperial Tobacco Company came to Pitt County and paid their state and county license tax of $1,000. On April 24, 1902, they bought a large tract of land along the Wilmington and Weldon Railroad from Charles T. Munford and his wife for $750. C.T. Munford was a leading merchant and land developer in Greenville who owned most of the land that became the tobacco district and named all the streets in that area.

In the first week of May 1902 work commenced on building the Imperial Tobacco factory. According to a feature on the factory in the local newspaper, H.J. Blauvelt of Richmond was the architect and Charles H. East of Danville, Virginia, was the contractor. The main building was to be two stories high measuring 65 by 200 feet, with a drying room 27 by 209 feet and a boiler house 40 by 50 feet. The plant was to be equipped with the latest improved machinery for handling tobacco and the company would hire from sixty to seventy workers, making them the largest employers in Greenville. Brick for the factory was shipped in by train and the Imperial Tobacco Company contracted for sand to be hauled from the sand mine near the river on Allen Warren's Riverside Nursery property. In late May, one of the men doing the hauling came near death when the walls of the mine collapsed on him, burying him to the top of his hat. A coworker quickly dug him out and he was not hurt, though badly frightened.

In late September 1902, it was a grand spectacle at the Imperial Tobacco Company to watch them raise a metal smokestack sixty feet long, thirty-two inches around and weighing 3,500 pounds onto a brick base. In March 1903 the tobacco plant was wired for electricity, the factory having been run on a dynamo battery. In the early morning of December 2, 1903, a terrible fire destroyed much of the tobacco district and the Imperial Tobacco Company was saved by great exertion, the fire burning only the fences and outbuildings. In March 1912, the metal smokestack fell across an adjacent building during a windstorm.

From late 1917 to August 1918, the Imperial Tobacco Company factory was enlarged with a huge addition, the work being done by D.J. Rose of Rocky Mount. It was enlarged with new storage buildings, a third story was added to the factory and the street in front of the factory was paved. Other additions included a two-story office building, with offices on the bottom and six bedrooms upstairs. A large brick smokestack 150 feet high and a 130,000-gallon water tank were also erected.

The Imperial Tobacco Company continued to expand in eastern North Carolina, having branch offices in Farmville, Washington, Williamston and Robersonville. In 1934, there was another huge addition to the Imperial Tobacco plant. According to the local newspaper "The Imperial plant, the largest redrying plant in the country, covers practically two city blocks, being about 600 feet long, 130 feet wide

This is a photograph of the office of the Imperial Tobacco Company built in 1918. The Imperial Tobacco Company operated in Greenville from 1903 to 1977 and had the largest tobacco processing plant in Greenville. *Courtesy of the author.*

and three stories in height. When working at full capacity this company can handle 400,000 pounds every twenty-four hours and they employ approximately 750 workers in the various departments."

In the evening of April 23, 1935, the tobacco town was again visited by another spectacular fire that destroyed numerous buildings. The Imperial Tobacco Company factory was threatened but withstood the fire. The Imperial office was badly damaged by both fire and water. One of the towering water tanks collapsed as the tremendous reservoir struck the ground, spilling thousands of gallons of water. For a time it was feared that the other water tank would also collapse, its girders weakened by the heat, but it remained standing.

Success led the Imperial Tobacco Company to again enlarge their plant in 1965, adding 43,500 square feet of storage space to handle more tobacco. But due to economic pressures in the market, Imperial made the decision to close the Greenville factory after seventy-four years and the building was sold in February 1978.

In 1981, Earl C. Wilson and his wife purchased the old tobacco plant to store recyclable plastics and renamed it the Greenville Storage and

Distribution Company. One more insult came on the evening of May 22, 1990, when the old Imperial Tobacco Company building caught fire and a twenty thousand-square foot portion of the building nearest Dickinson Avenue was destroyed. The design of the building and the fact that the firemen closed interior doors shortly after they arrived helped confine the fire to the southwest end of the building.

Whatever its future, the Imperial Tobacco Company building is an architectural treasure and a monument to the glory days of tobacco in Greenville's past.

Local Valentines Traditions

When it comes to Valentine's Day, everyone loves to get things like jewelry, candy or at least a card. But back about 1900, many a nervous person in Greenville couldn't wait until it was all over. Some of the old-timers in town can fondly recall the unusual local Valentine's traditions that looked more like Halloween.

Valentine's Day has long been a day for messages and tokens of love and adoration. But Victorian-era lovers needed no holiday to give tokens of affection. In many old Greenville families there have been found lockets and brooches containing some loved one's hair. There are also rings, necklaces, bracelets and pins featuring a snake with its tail in its mouth, which represented "eternal love." There are also pieces of jewelry containing pearls and moonstones. The moonstones were thought to give power over someone's love life and the pearls represented wisdom. Some of this early jewelry also employed a "secret code" to convey a message. The stones in this jewelry were arranged so that the first letter of the name of each stone spells out words like love, dearest or regards. Regards meant so much more then than it does now. We can sign a letter "best regards" and it doesn't mean we love that person. Back then, it meant you held that person in the very highest esteem.

Valentine's entertainment in Greenville consisted of the usual parties and an unusual amount of mischief by the boys. Old people said someone would carry a single handwritten party invitation to the door of each of the invited guests. Some of the parties were remembered as being masquerade parties with "love, cupid and the devil" represented in abundance. The local boys would turn St. Valentine's Day into a nuisance by tearing down signs and fence palings while carrying their valentines around in the evening. They would mix up their fun by raising a racket, breaking windows and carrying a club to bang on porches. The local newspaper would even warn people to tie up their bell cords by their front doors to keep them out of reach of the pranksters.

Perhaps the most unusual local tradition was the giving of insulting Valentines cards known as "penny-awfuls." These popular cards were sold at the Evans Book Store, which advertised that these cards "will show your secret spite."

Here are examples of the kind of cards that were passed around. The first is one that a young man might send to a young lady who didn't desire his companionship, entitled "A Conceited Nobody,"

> *You homely little strutting snip, about the streets you proudly trip*
> *as if you thought you were a peach, Pray have some sense, I do beseech!*
> *Your vanity must affect your sight, or your glass would tell you you're a fright!"*

The girl, being no slouch herself in the devastating Valentine department, would return the sentiment to "The Worst Tough and the Stupidest Dunce in the School,"

> *Here you are, you measly mite! Ain't you just a sickening sight?*
> *Dull and Lazy, tough and mean, The stupidest cub that can be seen!*
> *They ought to drown you, you worthless pup, Twill never pay to bring you up.*

Most of the cards of this type get right to the point. For example: "A Slob,"

> *Say, old girlie, fat and tough, at work you only make a bluff.*
> *You're a botch at every job; never was a worse old slob!*

Or "To a Face That Would Stop a Clock,"

> *In prison you ought to be doing some time, For to wear such a face must be purely a crime,*
> *If you 'mongst gorillas had chanced to be born, They would have disowned you with loathing and scorn;*

Local Valentines Tranditions

For a monkey—no matter how homely a brute, When placed beside you would be ranked as a "beaut."

Or "Why Don't You Teach Your Kids Some Manners?"

Precious set of kids you've got, The sauciest in the town;
For impudence and rudeness, They've won a great renown,
Amongst the lowest riff-raff, We'd surely have to go;
To find such vulgar breeding, As your young rowdies show!

The penny-awfuls faded away long ago, but their silly sentiment and imagination are more enjoyable than most cards seen today.

Tales from the Civil War

The following is a small group of collected stories concerning the Pitt County vicinity during the Civil War period. Some of the tales are humorous while others are examples of the spirit of the time.

Civil War Gun

In December 1909, Don L. Carson, while setting mink traps in Grindle Creek, discovered something in a hollow sweet gum tree. On investigation he found it to be a cylinder .44-caliber rifle with a barrel twenty-eight inches long. After talking to old people in the area, it was learned that the rifle was probably put there in about 1865 by a man named Thomas Crisp, a Confederate soldier who was run down by a posse of men and dogs and caught near where the gun was found. The gun bore marks that it had been used in the War of 1812. It was in a very good condition for having sat in a hollow tree for forty-three years. The gun could shoot six times and every barrel was loaded with big shot.

The Enemy's A'Coming

In May 1862, two companies of Confederates were stationed in Greenville. One night pickets came into town, alarming the town that the Yankees were advancing south of Greenville in force across a field belonging to Mr. Brown. The soldiers waited for the Yankees to appear and one company was ordered to retreat across the river. The other company formed themselves upon one hill in Greenville in line of battle. The idea was to give the Yankees a volley from their double-barrel guns. Then the Confederates were to retreat and save themselves as best they could. In the meantime, they had sent a squad in advance to give warning of the approach of the enemy. The squad went as far as Brown's field where, lo and behold, they spied the enemy that the pickets had heard advancing in force across the field. The enemy turned out to be a drove of cattle foraging in the field, and the whole alarm turned out to be in the imagination of the picket's brain.

Civil War Melon

J.H. Barnhill of House, Pitt County, reported in 1902 that in 1865 he grew a muskmelon or cantaloupe that weighed forty pounds and that one man sat down and ate half of it at one sitting.

Pitt County Heroine

Amid the dark days of the Civil War when food was scarce and everything seemed to be at a point of desolation, the dread disease smallpox broke out in the army. A young soldier from North Carolina was placed as guard at an improvised hospital in Virginia.

One day while seated near the gate, the guard looked around and saw an approaching form, a gigantic woman or what seemed more likely a man in woman's apparel. The coarse homespun dress was nothing strange for the times, but the masculine appearance and the huge form awakened something akin to fear as the strange looking woman passed in front of him and asked in a deep voice, "Is Skilton Dennis in there?" The guard replied, "Yes, he is in there."

"Then open the gate."

"No one is allowed to pass here except certain ones detailed for hospital duty. I am here to see that no one goes in or comes out without a pass."

At this reply, the woman reached down into a pocket and drew therefrom a long, gleaming knife, saying, "If Skilton Dennis is in there, I am going in if I have to wade through blood knee-deep."

The steamboats *Tar River* and *Shiloh* are shown moored to the wharf at Boyd's Ferry, Pitt County, waiting for enough water to steam upriver. *Courtesy of North Carolina Archives.*

With his hair rising and without another word, the guard opened the gate and Miss Ruthie Dennis of Pitt County, North Carolina, walked through. Miss Dennis stayed for many days trying to aid the sick, and when her brother was well enough, she and he departed for home. Outwardly rough and unattractive, inwardly she was remembered as a soul of mercy. Miss Ruthie Dennis lived near Ayden, North Carolina, and her brother Skilton Dennis has descendants still living in Pitt County.

Finding Tar River

During the Civil War when the Confederates evacuated Washington, North Carolina, they rolled one thousand barrels of tar and turpentine into the Tar River at Taft's Store in Pitt County. Two months later a steamboat, the *Colonel Hill*, with four hundred Yankee prisoners going from Salisbury, North Carolina, to Washington to be exchanged, tied up at the wharf at Taft's Store to let the boys bathe. When all the men got in the water, they stirred up the tar on the bottom of the river and were smeared with it from head to toe. When they got out of the water, each man was given his ration of meat in one hand and a small stick for scraping in the other. When asked, "What's the matter?" the Yankees replied, "Durned if we haven't found Tar River at last; the whole riverbed is covered with pitch!"

Fled the Draft

In June 1871, a local newspaper reported the following strange story. It was reported that a man named Edward Brown of Pitt County fled to the swamps during the late war to avoid the draft and had lately been discovered living a hermit's life in a den and settlement in a dense thicket near the bank of the river. When first discovered he fled to his hiding place. Upon being pursued he showed fight, but finally surrendered and insisted he would not go into the army. Upon being informed that the war had ended about six years before, he concluded to abandon his hiding place and return to the old plantation, where he found many changes since the commencement of the rebellion. His only clothing was made from the skins of coons and other animals that he had captured during his time hiding. He had not seen or spoken to anyone for about eight years, and he had nearly lost the control of language except for a few profane words. His father and mother had both died during the past year.

Rambling in the 1960s: Entertainment in Greenville

Thinking back about the 1960s may seem too recent to be considered history, but forty years have passed and much has been forgotten. So let's jog our memories a little as we remember some of the local nightspots and entertainment in Greenville.

We'll start back in January 1963, when the Rathskeller, known as "the Rat," was opened at 109 East Fifth Street (the former Sharky's). The owners were Jim Cheatham, Roger Mann and Lynn Stinson. It had a "continental atmosphere" with a rustic German décor designed by Stinson. The Rathskeller catered to businessmen for lunch and had a lounge and tavern. Later it is remembered as serving mainly beer, pizza and sandwiches. An interesting footnote is that on the evening of January 23, 1963, the night before the formal opening of the place, Dave Brubeck of New York jazz fame was giving a concert at East Carolina. After the concert, he and actress-singer Jane Morgan, an avid fan who was also at the concert, partied at the Rathskeller.

In the spring of 1964, the owners of the Rathskeller leased an old fishing vessel permanently beached on the Atlantic Beach Causeway, known as the Barnacle, as a nightclub. In May 1965 the Rathskeller opened its patio known as "the Marquis" for rock and roll. The Rathskeller went out of business sometime in the early 1980s.

In September 1964, the Purple and Gold Club opened for East Carolina students and guests on the 264 bypass in the old Cinderella Restaurant (later Sweet Caroline's). The Purple and Gold Club offered full-course meals and nightly dancing to the jukebox. It closed in October 1964. Also in September 1964, R.W. Griffin opened a club known as the Tortugas Club over his Buccaneer Restaurant on the corner of Fifth and Evans Streets. The Tortugas was for East Carolina students and their guests only. He later called it the Hideaway in November 1965. It is unknown when the club closed.

In December 1964 the Alpha Phi Omega fraternity opened its own "private club" when the college banned parties at fraternities. This club, known as the Tavern, was an upstairs room in back of Campus Corner, a clothing store at the corner of Fifth and Cotanche Streets. The Tavern had a bar and featured dancing every weekend.

Probably the most fantastic club in Greenville was one on Dickinson Avenue known as the Castaway Club. It was advertised as "Collegiate Carolina's Number One Club" and from the many national headliners that appeared there, it was. The club was incorporated on September 15, 1965, with B.E. Griffin, John E. Mulston Jr. and M.G. Bateman as owners. It opened on October 1, 1965, for couples only; no one under eighteen was admitted and ties were required. The list of groups that played there was outstanding, with bands such as Little Anthony and the Imperials, Martha and the Vandellas, Maurice Williams and the Zodiacs, Mary Wells and Orchestra, the Enchanters, Doug Clark and the Hot Nuts, the Dixie Cups, the Tropics, Chester Mayfield and the Casuals, the Dazzlers, Little David and the Wanderers, the Sensations, the Steps of Rhythm, the Tams, the Toys and the O'Kaysions. The O'Kaysions were from Wilson, North Carolina, and it has been said that their number one hit, "I'm a Girl Watcher," was first recorded at the Castaway Club. The Castaway Club had trouble with its beer permits and eventually closed. Its incorporation was suspended on September 4, 1969.

On December 9, 1965, the Coach and Four restaurant and nightclub opened on Cotanche Street (where the Elbo Room is). It was owned by Paul Hersh, Stanton Taylor, Thurman Jackson and Earl Kaykandall. They offered food, fun and entertainment in an Old English setting. In July 1967 they had two go-go girls in a cage that created a sensation, but local authorities made them appear with more clothes on. When the Coach and Four ended is unknown, but the Elbo was there by 1970.

In October 1966 a new club known as Bob's Barn opened at Play Meadows, a half mile north of Greenville on North Greene Street, behind the old Riverside Oyster Bar. Bob's Barn could accommodate one thousand people and 90 percent of its business came from college students. Bob's Barn had such entertainment as the Jokers 7, Mary

This 1960s postcard view shows Evans Street looking north in Greenville. This is the way so many people remember Evans Street before the walking mall was built in 1976. Now Evans Street is open again to traffic and the downtown is coming to life again. *Courtesy of Judy Nobles Lewis*

Wells, the Prophets, Freddie and the Soul Twisters, Bobby Dee and the Mad Hatters and Mr. Lee Fields (known as James Brown Jr.).

Other nightspots on the outskirts of Greenville were Ruby's Circle Y Restaurant and Drive-In on the Pactolus highway at the intersection of Routes 30 and 33. Ruby's had a live band every Saturday night. Another was the Country Place, located eight miles from Greenville. It opened in early 1967 and had dancing on weekends.

The most notable country place was the beautiful Candlewick Inn, located on the Stantonsburg Road. The Candlewick had dancing on weekends and served food and alcohol in an elegant setting.

In the way of other entertainment, there were four motion picture theaters in the area: The Meadowbrook Picture Theatre, the Pitt, the State and the Tice Drive-In. The Tice was located on the Ayden highway.

For billiard fans there were two pool halls located in downtown Greenville—Happy's Pool Room and Pop's Billiards.

Several nightspots in Greenville were associated with churches. The Catacombs, which was located in the basement of the Methodist

Student Center, had food and live entertainment on Fridays and Saturdays. The Presbyterian Church also sponsored two spots in town, the Den, a supper and conversation club, and the Itch, which was a coffeehouse open on Thursdays for married couples and on weekends for college students.

Most people who know something about Greenville know that Robert Saieed and his brother George Saieed are identified heavily with entertainment downtown. Early on, Robert Saieed had a restaurant known as the Varsity, and later he opened a small one on East Fifth Street known as the Bohemian (where the former Subway was). He redecorated it and the New Bohemian opened in January 1970.

In late 1966, the Saieeds opened a large restaurant, tap room and dance hall known as Fiddlers III across the street from the Bohemian. The Fiddlers III restaurant seated 190 people; the taproom, 120; and the upstairs dance hall and bar, 500. The interior was designed in a European style by Robert Edminston of the East Carolina School of Art. The restaurant opened in October 1966 with the bands the Sting Rays and the Inmates. They had their grand opening on January 22, 1967.

The upstairs dance hall was first called the Place to Be Above the Fiddlers III. It featured soul and beach music on the jukebox during the week and bands on Saturday nights. In the summer of 1968, the dance hall changed its name to the ID, which had a psychedelic atmosphere with black lights, strobe lights, mirror balls and the sounds of hard rock, acid rock and rock and roll.

In September 1971, Tom Haines became manager of the nightspot and the name changed to the Attic. It opened to the public on September 8, 1971. The décor was changed to natural ecology featuring rough wood furniture, and the music changed to bluegrass, blues-rock and some road shows. They also offered the first foosball tables in Greenville. In January 1976, the Attic moved to the old Buccaneer Club on Fourth Street. The Attic burned on September 9, 1984, and was moved again to the King and Queen Restaurant building across the river. The Attic eventually came home and the rest is history.

Groups that appeared at the Fiddlers III dance hall included the Markels, the Entertainers, Capris', the Wreck of the Old '97, Ben King, the Tams, Lee Dorsey, Timmy Willis and the Checkmates, Bobby Moore and the Rhythm Aces, the Box Tops, the Soul, Ltd. and the Huckleberry Mudflaps.

The Fiddlers III Restaurant closed in 1975 and reopened on January 15, 1976, as the Jolly Roger dance club. It later became Rafters and is now the Cellar.

One of the local bands mentioned above, the Wreck of the Old '97, was a popular local group that played in a number of clubs. The Wreck were five unshaven young men touted as the "Dean of Women's Nightmares" and consisted of Bobby Paul, John Tuttle, Tim Hildebrandt, Steve Sullins and Tommy Steele. They played rock, reggae and rhythm and blues.

In October 1967, a club opened at 103 East Fourth Street known as the Ruins. The club had a unique interior, like old Roman ruins, and is remembered for having the first house band downtown, known as the Gypsy Moths. The Ruins went out of business by September 1968 but the club reopened in October 1968 as the Buccaneer Club. The Buc had its grand opening on October 25, 1968, with the New York Sounds (of Funky Broadway fame) as the first headliner. The Buccaneer soon became "the South's Third Largest Beach Music Club" with the Embers playing there every other Thursday night. Behind the Buccaneer Club was later another small place known as the Windjammer Disco. The Buccaneer Club closed by December 1975. In January 1976, the Attic moved into the old Buccaneer Club building until it burned in 1984. An obscure party place called Ye Old Jail Tavern opened in April 1969. Ye Old Jail Tavern became a favorite fraternity drinking spot. It was located down on the Tar River near the sandpits behind the airport.

In January 1971, the Music Factory opened in a warehouse on the corner of Fourteenth and Cotanche Streets. The Music Factory advertised big-name headliners, but appears to have only lasted a short while. As a footnote, the tobacco warehouse on the corner of Charles and Fourteenth Streets was the site of the Greenville appearance of the King of Funk, James Brown, back in May 1965.

Certainly one of the most familiar nightspots downtown was the aforementioned Elbo Room, which opened on November 15, 1968, with little fanfare. The original Elbo Room opened one-fourth the size it became by 1995, consisting of a small bar, two pinball machines and one small bathroom split into two. The limited, confined space prompted the owners to call it the Elbo Room.

The Elbo Room was started by Joey Allen McGroarty and a partner. Other owners over the years include Dennis Dale Bercinin, James M. Roberts, John Banks, Mike Beulow and Kirby Bryson. With the different owners and changes over the years, many people will remember the bands that played there in the '70s and their house band, Steel Rail.

Another almost forgotten dance place in the '60s was the Bel-Air Club. It was located out on Hooker Road where Wilson-Rhodes Electrical Contractors have their office. It appears to go back to 1959 and was at its popularity peak in 1964. It is said to have been a nice place, only open on weekends. They had bands on Friday nights and a DJ and records on Saturday night. Some people still remember "bopping to the Beatles at the Bel-Air."

Another unique entertainment place in town was known as PGI, which opened in July 1965. It was located at Colonial Heights on both sides of East Tenth Street and advertised itself as having the first indoor putt-putt course in the United States. Where it was located is unknown, though some people believed it was where the ECU Harris Building is, across from the old Pizza Hut on Tenth Street.

And so, I come to the end of our rambling except to mention some local entertainers. Some people will remember a local female trio known as the Tonettes back in 1966 and Little Eva and her smash hit "Locomotion" back in 1965. She was from Plymouth, North Carolina.

I hope you have enjoyed our sojourn into the 1960s in Greenville. Who could forget that the minimum wage was one dollar an hour, the national debt was only $300 billion, Brook Valley Country Club opened in 1966, Star Trek changed television in 1966, car phones came to Greenville in 1968 and the most popular pastime was "Monstervision" at the local theater.

Tales of the Halloween Season

Halloween is that time of year when the trees begin to turn again in the warm light of fall and thoughts turn to strange stories of "goblins, boogers and haints." Halloween, once considered a harmless fancy, has now become quite a commercial venture. But many years ago Halloween was celebrated quite differently.

According to T.C. Davis in 1909, Halloween in Greenville before the Civil War was a day on which our staid ancestors would gather for a vigil, or watch night, for works of charity and to visit the graves of their passed loved ones. At early dawn, many people would attend their churches to celebrate communion or what was then called "All Saints Day," to remember their beloved dead.

But certainly the most tantalizing part of the Halloween season is the stories and tales of things that are unexplainable. Here below is an excerpt of a narrative from the 1930s about strange things the author of the narrative had heard about Pitt County when he was young.

> *When I was much younger, I used to enjoy sitting around a hot wood-stove, listening to the black tenant farmers on my fathers farm weave their stories of "haints" and some of the unexplainable things seen by their parents in the old days.*
>
> *After hearing these stories over and over again I began to wonder if they were not true. Even so, I often wondered why I had never seen anything. When I mentioned this they would say, "Why child you ain't never going to see 'em if you don't believe."*

One of the tenants would not plow in the "Island Field," a field about a mile or more in the backwoods, after the sun started setting. He told my father that one day he saw "something white" coming out of the swamp toward him about dark and that his mule got so scared that he broke the traces and ran. Sometime afterward another tenant said someone or something called his name clearly several times while he was working in the field late one day.

I dispersed that thought from my mind, thinking they were imagining things, until something strange happened to me. One afternoon I was plowing in an island field just as the sun set and having only two or three rows left decided to continue. A few minutes after the sun went down over the trees someone called my name, faint at first but clearer the second and third time.

The sound was getting louder and clearer as I continued to plow. Presently my mule began to get uneasy and started to snort. I decided to leave without an explanation for the incident.

When I got back to the stables, I told the tenant what had happened and he confirmed that it always happens around that time of day.

A favorite story of mine is that of an old man who once lived on the farm who talked about "the thing" he saw pass him on a lonely swamp road about dusk one night. He swore that he heard something coming up behind him and he turned around to see what it was and a human on all fours passed him loping like a dog.

Another man said he was walking along the same road late one night by himself and a man without a head passed him. According to the way he used to tell the story, the "thing" never slowed up and soon disappeared when it got a short distance from him.

This old Creek Road, famous to the black farmers living in the general area of my father's farm, had many more stories told about it. Back in the old days "something" used to get on carriages and wagons near the Creek Bridge and weigh it down so the horse could not move. One old white man said he was riding alone when "a thing" hitched a ride with him and rode for about a half mile before disappearing.

Some of the older men and women said they used to hear a "death ring" in their ear and right after it they would hear about someone dying. One old white woman told my father she saw my grandmother about an hour after she died and that she came up to her window and called her by name.

The night after my grandmother died, several heard the big bell at the homeplace (which called to the field workers) ring continuously. Another saw a huge light in the trees surrounding the house.

Many strange stories I have heard around a woodstove. Who can actually say they are not true?

Images of Pitt County

Macon G. Moye and his family proudly stand in front of their house and show off their car known as a "Hupmobile." The house formerly stood on the site of Chicos Restaurant on South Memorial Drive, Winterville. *Courtesy of Buddy Waters.*

A group of Pitt County hunters show off their trophy before the camera in the late 1910s. The only known hunters include Ola Forbes (left) and his sons (two on the right) and Addison Monroe Waters (third from left). *Courtesy of Buddy Waters.*

The Bertha Hotel, built in 1900 on Fifth Street by Ben F. Patrick, was the first commercial hotel in Greenville. In 1917, the Bertha Hotel became known as the Princeton Hotel. It burned in 1925 and the Princeton Hotel moved to a building on the corner of Greene Street and Dickinson Avenue. The Bertha Hotel building housed the A&P Store in 1925. *Courtesy of Illustrated City of Greenville, 1914.*

The beautiful Proctor Hotel sat on the southwest corner of Evans and Third Streets, diagonal from the courthouse. The hotel opened in 1913 as the second commercial hotel in Greenville. It is interesting to note that stunt men would climb the outside of the building in the 1930s and, during World War II, Proctor Hotel towels were spotted all over the Pacific. *Courtesy of Judy Nobles Lewis.*

This view from 1914 shows all the businesses on Evans Street looking north from above Five Points. The first pay phone in Greenville was located at Bryan and Nichols Drug Store in 1901. During World War I and World War II merchants had to turn off their electric signs to conserve fuel and if they forgot they were fined by the fuel administrator. *Courtesy of Illustrated City of Greenville, 1914.*

Above: This view from 1914 shows Evans Street looking south from Third Street. The Proctor Hotel is on the left and the *Daily Reflector* office is on the right. Evans Street was first paved with brick in 1908 from Third Street to Five Points and then out Dickinson Avenue to the depot. *Courtesy of Illustrated City of Greenville, 1914.*

Opposite above: This view from about 1917 shows the first school bus in Pitt County. The bus was purchased when the Craft School and Falkland district schools combined in 1917. The sides could be rolled down to protect the children during foul weather. *Courtesy of the North Carolina Collection, J.Y. Joyner Library, East Carolina University.*

Below: A crowd has assembled in 1917 in front of the schoolhouse in Falkland, Pitt County, to admire the new school bus. *Courtesy of the North Carolina Collection, J.Y. Joyner Library, East Carolina University.*

Standing out in front of the William Moye house (left to right) are Walter James, William Moye (1863–1927) and his third wife, Mary E. Parker, and his child William Elbert Moye; Mrs. Winnie Parker Forbes and son, Peter Forbes. The two girls are Alice and Nannie Moye, daughters of William Moye. The house formerly sat on what is now Greenville Boulevard Southwest, by Tobacco Road. The house was later moved to Winterville. *Courtesy of John F. Moye.*

The Noah Forbes Jr. and wife Martha Tucker home and family as it appeared in 1900. Family members pictured (left to right) are Betty, Bertha, Walter, Edward, Pearl, Martha, Noah, Nora, Neva, Nannie, C. Heber and Clara Forbes. The house sat where the Carolina East Convenience Center now sits and was moved to the Allen Road by John F. Moye. *Courtesy of John F. Moye.*

About the Author

Roger Kammerer is an artist and local historian in Greenville, North Carolina. He grew up on the coast in Swansboro, North Carolina, where he gained his love for North Carolina history and research under the tutelage of the renowned North Carolina historian, Tucker Reed Littleton. He came to East Carolina University in Greenville on an art scholarship in 1974 and has remained in Greenville ever since. Roger has written his "Pitt's Past" column for the *Greenville Times* since 1984. He has authored or co-authored twenty books and booklets on local records and genealogy. In 2001, he and Candace Pearce published a photographic book on Greenville, which contained over two hundred images. He is a member of the Pitt County Historical Society, the Pitt County Family Researchers and the East Carolina Village of Yesteryear. Besides giving talks and walking tours, he contributes his art and history to many local publications.

Visit us at
www.historypress.net

www.ingramcontent.com/pod-product-compliance
Lightning Source LLC
Chambersburg PA
CBHW060811100426
42813CB00004B/1029